I REMEMBER: INDIANAPOLIS YOUTH WRITE ABOUT THEIR LIVES

2021

DAROLYN "LYN" JONES

I REMEMBER

Indianapolis Youth Write About Their Lives

2021

10th Volume

Edited by Darolyn "Lyn" Jones

Cover Design by Andrea Boucher

Interior Layout by Darolyn "Lyn" Jones and University Student Interns: Danilo Almeida and Sarah Seyfried

Editing Assistance: Kelsey Johnson, Devon Lejman, and Emily Mack

University Student Intern Editor: Sarah Seyfried

Indiana Writers Center "Building a Rainbow" Youth Public Memoir Project

Executive Director

Rachel Sahaidachny

Writer in Residence

Barbara Shoup

Education Outreach Director

Dr. Darolyn "Lyn" Jones

Program Director

Sarah Ginter

INDIANA WRITERS CENTER

Thank you to our generous funders and donors.

WESTMINSTER Neighborhood Services, Inc

goose THE MARKET

HORIZONS
St. Richard's Episcopal School

Saint Florian Center

THE CITY OF INDIANAPOLIS
MAYOR JOE HOGSETT
EST. 1921

DO Something Positive
BE Someone Positive
HAVE Something Positive

amazon literary partnership

ARTSCOUNCIL

Summer Youth Program Fund

ABC Teachers' Treasures
Helping Teachers Help Kids!

NATIONAL ENDOWMENT for the ARTS
arts.gov

ALLEN WHITEHILL CLOWES CHARITABLE FOUNDATION

INDIANA ARTS COMMISSION

LILLY ENDOWMENT ◆INC◆

Table of Contents

Building a Rainbow

Funded by the Summer Youth Program Fund (SYPF), as well as generous foundation, corporate and individual donors, the Indiana Writers Center's "Building a Rainbow" creative writing program serves a diverse group of young people at three Indianapolis sites: St. Florian Youth Leadership Camp, Westminster Neighborhood Center, and Horizons at St. Richard's School. The program is named after a colorful, whimsical poster of a half-made rainbow that is covered with tiny stick figures painting, hammering and operating cranes as they work to finish it. The image is a visual reminder that there are many small steps in creating something beautiful—a piece of writing, a dream a goal, a life.

Working one-on-one, IWC instructors, student interns, and volunteers help the young writers improve their writing and literacy skills through a series of creative writing exercises that teach them how to write the stories of their own lives. They also encourage them to reflect upon the experiences they've written about, considering how what they've learned can help them make their dreams come true.

———

After more than a year of anxiety, isolation, and very little fun, my world burst into full color on the June day our summer learning program began. I didn't know how much I'd missed the children we work with until—there they were! So young and beautiful and full of life that for the first time in a long while it seemed to me that things were going to be okay. If the world is ever going to right itself, I thought, these young people are the ones who are going to make it happen.

I love this program! I love seeing children, heads bent, concentrating hard, writing as fast as they can to make the pictures in their heads into words. I love talking to a child who's stuck, asking questions, making suggestions, maybe even writing a few sentences for her until something in her face changes and she reaches for the pencil to continue her story herself. I love those moments when the program is working just as it should and a certain kind of quiet falls over the room because the children are all lost in the worlds inside their heads. I love how they so often surface, proud and often surprised by what they've written.

I love the stories they write! I'm often moved to tears by the honesty with which they write about the world and their lives in it: the reality of racism, the particulars of loss, the loneliness and frustration of Covid quarantine. Stories about the people they love, their best days, and favorite things never fail to delight me. I appreciate the respectful way they listen to one another read their work, share what they like, ask questions, and make connections to their own experiences.

Our students make me remember how much I believe in the power of young people to see things as they really are and to help us see them in ways we've forgotten.

Here are their stories. I know you will read them with pleasure and amazement.

Barbara Shoup
Writer-in-Residence
Indiana Writers Center

From the Editorial and Educational Outreach Director

———

We at the Indiana Writers Center have been lifting up youth voices that are pushed down since 2009 when we started a youth memoir project at the Girl's Federal Prison in Indianapolis, Indiana. After that project, we knew this kind of truth telling was what we should be doing all of the time. And so, the project began.

In the early years and inception of this project, we faced resistant wardens, guards, and a lockdown. And yet every week, those girls protested that resistance by showing up hungry to put their stories on paper. And that was equally true this summer.

This summer our resistance was to the widespread pandemic deaths that impacted our local communities, violence in the streets, protests and peaceful marches for #blacklivesmatter, eviction notices, a living wage, lack of food and medical care, and a year of no or limited access to technology. This summer, more than *any* other summer, is when our students needed *us* the most and needed words the most. They needed to make meaning and make sense on paper of what they were hearing, seeing, experiencing this past year and even now as the country tries to recover and heal. They needed to make meaning and make sense of their anger, their loneliness, their confusion, their resistance, their fear, their questions. And they needed us to help them with that.

All of our sites met face-to-face. Yet, the pandemic isn't over. We remained masked and physically distanced. Our usual number of students of 200 to 250 was reduced to 140 because of city spacing requirements and families still unsure if their child would be safe meeting in person with others. We adapted. We did everything and anything we could to let our young writers know that we loved them, we supported them, and they could trust us with their stories.

Last year was to be our 10th volume of this book, *I Remember: Indianapolis Youth Write About Their Lives*, but sadly, Covid prevented that. So, while this is our 11th year with this program, it is our 10th volume edition. What the students wrote, and what we are delivering to you in this 10th volume will make you marvel at how brilliantly and beautifully their brains buoy. Their words should make you angry and cry at the pain on the paper. Their words should make you smile and laugh at the joy you witness in the everyday practices that only children do—you know, the ones we don't do anymore as adults and have long forgotten, but the ones that once reminded, we would do anything to go back and relive just one more time. Their words should move you. You should be changed after you read this collection.

At the 2020 Indiana Black Expo Educators Conference, I heard Dr. Marc Lamont-Hill speak, and he urged young people to be radical, restorative, and to have a true freedom dream. I hope when you read this collection, you can hear their radical and restorative freedom voices telling you that #blacklivesmatter, that black boy and girl joy is real, that learning online is something they loved or hated, that they have suffered loss, about what makes them laugh, about their hopes and dreams, and that they find joy in learning how to swim, play basketball, and being a trickster.

Here is what we tell them/teach them to encourage them to write their stories and speak their truths.

- This isn't school. This isn't English class. In these workshops (not classes), we will learn and write like writers. Don't worry about spelling, mechanics, or grammar. That's what editors are for.
- Writing comes from the head, heart, and gut. But good writing comes from the heart and gut, *especially* the gut.
- We believe you have a story to tell. You are the expert of your life and your story, and your story matters. And if

you don't tell your story, somebody else may tell it for you, and tell it wrong.

- We will remember and create a picture in the reader's head so the reader can see and imagine what it's like to live and walk in our shoes.
- We are writing for an audience. This book will be published. Hundreds, even thousands will hear your truths.
- When you write, Write Loud and Proud.
- We share our writing during Author's Chair, which has three simple rules: Read Loud and Proud, Listen Quietly, and No Judging. And If you don't want to share or publish what we wrote, you don't have to. You are the author. You own your words. You decide which stories to write, tell, and publish.
- Writing is composed. It is not written; it is not crafted. And everyone has the capacity to create and to imagine. People who write new music for songs or for instruments are called composers. To create new sounds, composers order sounds and then dispose of sounds creating a melody, and then they place multiple sounds together simultaneously to create harmony. Music compositions are built until the sound is pleasing to the composer. You are not just physically writing words, nor are you only crafting or weaving, you are creating a cacophony of words, voice, rhythm, and details that deliver a message (Baumann and Jones, 2020).
- And finally, there are many small steps in building anything—a dream, a piece of writing, a life.

I am a writer. And I teach creative narrative nonfiction writing both at the Indiana Writers Center and at Ball State University. But, there is something so incredibly special and poignant about young writers. Unlike adult learners, they are unfiltered and unschooled and unafraid to write from the gut. They literally laugh out loud when they write, break down in tears, and sometimes have to stop because it's too painful. We hear and witness what most folks have never or would never. Our instructors, interns, and volunteers tell us that working with these young writers makes them better writers, better teachers, better humans. It's why we all come back every summer. And every summer, I worry about whether or not we will have enough money for supplies or to pay our instructors and interns a small stipend. And yet, every summer, donations roll in.

This is a longer letter than I normally write, because reflecting back on these 11 years, I'm feeling so much, but mostly I'm feeling purpose and pride and gratitude. I take great pride and have found great purpose in helping young writers tell their truths. Cliché as it sounds, I feel gratitude in knowing that young people learn from us and that they, again, trust us. For the last 11 years, we have delivered the message that young people's stories matter. We have come far, but we will continue to build and grow because there is still so much more we can do.

Thank you, young writers, for trusting us with your stories.

Thank you, instructors, interns, and volunteers for teaching, transcribing, creating, and serving. This program wouldn't work without you.

Thank you to our funders and donation givers. Without you, we couldn't continue to provide the supplies and tools that allow us feed our students words and food.

Thank you to the Indiana Writers Center for continuing to believe in this program.

Finally, thank you, to my mentor, friend, and partner in this program, Writer in Residence, Barbara Shoup.

Now, join me in this special concord of voices singing to you from the page.

Dr. Darolyn "Lyn" Jones
    Education Outreach Director,
    Indiana Writer's Center

Baumann, M. & Jones, D.L. (2020). Unschooling teaching practices and community literacy. *Journal of Teaching Writing, 35*(2), 59-108.

Horizons Program at St. Richard's Episcopal School

One of my favorite prompts this summer was inspired by George Ella Lyon's poem "I Come From". In it, the speaker describes black dirt under the back porch of her childhood home that "tasted like beets".

When they heard this line, our third and fourth grade students were appalled and asked, "How did she know what it tasted like? Did she *eat* the dirt?"

"Maybe!" we said.

Each Tuesday and Thursday in the sunny library at the Horizons Program held at Saint Richard's School, our students shared with us where *they* come from.

They come from mom's spaghetti, Auntie's gumbo, sticky cotton candy on the Fourth of July, or a candy bar split with a friend on the playground.

They come from Nanas who learn TikTok dances, brothers and sisters who pull pranks, and teachers who believe in them.

They come from friends who keep secrets, and friends who don't.

They come from the pride and excitement of learning to swim or getting cool new shoes.

They come from the heartbreak of losing a parent or grandparent.

We—instructors and interns— came prepared with colored pencils, notebooks, and inspiration from poets like Maya Angelou, Eloise Greenfield, and George Ella Lyon. But our students came with their experiences, their imaginations, their enthusiasm, and their unfiltered honesty.

After an unusual and isolating year of teaching and learning through a screen, it was a pure joy to look into their eyes, to see their heads bent over a physical notebook page in concentration, to hear them laugh and say *"Uh-huh!"* and snap for each other's stories read aloud.

It is an honor to be allowed these beautiful glimpses into their lives.
It is an honor to be trusted with their stories.

Emily Mack
Co-Instructor at Horizons Program

Aiza K.
Age 9

A Beautiful Dream

I see myself in a beautiful forest, and I walk around to discover flowers made out of gems. They feel edgy. I hear unicorns neighing. I run to the unicorns and pet two of them. They feel soft. I see an apple made out of gems. I feed it to them. They enjoy it. They all start to run away.

Aiza K.
Age 9

I Come From

I am from Pakistan
I am from my family celebrating Eid
I am from my family celebrating Ramadan
I am from Pakistan bread the sweetest
I am from Rosea
I am from Hijabs
I am from my family's heart
I am from the world
I am from Allah

Camari B.
Age 10

Peace

You should know that I got bullied for six whole years. It is over, but still buried in my brain. It was sad. I had nothing to do about that, but is it really okay now? Idk, but I have peace and quiet now. No talking about how I look or having fake friends or none of that. I feel better about myself, but having anger issues is not good. Still at least, I have family and friends. I like my aunt and grandfather. He is in heaven now, so he can watch me from down here. It's cool when they call me, and we talk for like an hour or so. It's fun and I feel like I need them in my life. They are my one and only.

Camari B.
  Age 10

I Come From

I live in Gary in Indiana, an old place where family lives peacefully in peace. Corn made truthfully by grandmother; cousins getting in trouble by running in the halls. It's fun, but old.

Going to church every single Sunday. Maybe, just maybe, God will come around. Traveling with mum where I got the British saying from. It's fun but old.

It's the Juneteenth celebration, drinking spilling juice and having fun. Wearing twirly dresses and pretty shoes. It's fun but old.

Aunt Gena Cuzin Maliya and Grandma: Grandmothers making biscuits— yes, yes delicious. Beautiful as can be, the ocean fish swimming in a crowd we all hug family like us. It's fun but old.

Christian P.
  Age 8

The Friend

Everyday at Pleasant Run school, my friend is mean. She always wants something. I always bring a candy bar or a Nutrigrain bar in my lunchbox. My friend always wants it, but then I wouldn't have anything to eat. I want to stop being friends with her, but I was too scared. The next day I finally built up the courage, and said *I don't wanna be friends.* The end!

Christian P.
  Age 8

The Shoes

Every day my dad makes colorful shoes. Last time I made my own shoes. I put stars and diamonds with neon colors. First, you have to put the diamonds and stars. Then you have to put tape where you can't color. Finally, you need to color around the stars and diamonds. After I did that, my dad did the rest.

Danny H.
  Age 9

The Mysterious Footprint?

It was quiet as I walked up the stairs, a foot print followed. I walked in my room and saw a bunch of small footprints on the walls and on the bed. I was scared and hid under my blankets, then I hear something in my closet. I then fell asleep...and woke up. My sister then told me that she did the footprint prank.

Danny H.
  Age 9

I Can't Breathe

The song "I Can't Breathe" by Dax makes me feel about Covid and makes me feel grateful. I'm grateful because I didn't die to Covid. I'm also grateful because my family did not die. The song "I Can't Breathe" will always make me remember about me and my family and how we survived.

E.J.
    Age 9

Water Wars

I was at the water park, and I splashed water on this kid a bunch of times. And then the kid's brother or cousin looked up and while the kid was pointing to me, I saw the water gun and he started to spray me nonstop. And when he was done, I splashed the kid again. But this time, there were two other boys came and got me. After that I gave up. Or that's what they thought.

E.J.
    Age 9

Love

I love drawing, filling lots of pages.
    I love beatboxing, practicing every day.
    I love Pokemon, organizing my cards.
    I love being funny, making everyone in my
    class laugh.
    I love Ritchie, he is my friend.

Emani T.
    Age 10

I Am From

I'm from Alabama. We eat hot dogs and the kids got candy and ice cream and the adults got adult juice. And I loved the hot dog my Titi got us. We got some more ice cream. And my Titi made us some cake and I got more cake, and I got some cake mix. And me and my dad got some candy. I got to see my mom. I was going to stay, but I was tired, but my mom didn't care. My mom got me, and I got up and I was confused and I didn't know where I was. I saw my sister. She ran to me and hugged me. She told my mom she was happy to see me up and my Titi was happy to see me. Me and my sisters went to the park. We got to see my favorite Aunt. She cried in happy.

Emani T.
  Age 10

I Love You...

I love going on rides in the car.
  The last time we went on a ride
  We went to the movies
  We saw *Black Panther*.
  I love my brother
  We look just alike but some people be like
  "Are you guys twins?"
  We are like "No."
  I love Sky Zone
  It is so green and we got on the zipline.

Gracie J.
  Age 10

Like/Don't Like

  I like to play football,
  I love to play Fortnite,
  I don't like to write,
  I don't like my brother,
  I like to play ball and to cook

Gracie J.
  Age 10

A Week Without Fortnite

The day I did not play Fortnite for a week. So my dad said if I did not play Fortnite for a week, he will give me 100 dollars in V-bucks and then he will go get me a dog. So I was on TikTok for the whole week. I was bored and I got 100 dollars in V-bucks and a dog, so I was so happy that I did it. I got a motorcycle and we got dinner. We got a baby dog and I named it Jeffy and it is a boy and I have a girl dog already. So I have two dogs and I have a lot of dollars!

Hayyaan M.
  Age 8

Guitar

I like the way a guitar sounds. I tried to learn to play. When I tried to play, it was very hard. It was hard to get the right notes. I would press the wrong string and mess the whole thing up. I tried to play a song called "Snowman". I practiced for one day. Every time I messed up, I gave up the next day. Maybe I'll go back to playing guitar, but with a different song.

Hayyaan M.
  Age 8

I Am From

I am from Pakistan.
It is mostly
peaceful. I'm a bird, peaceful
As I am fast as wind. We have
Foods we like. I am a
Person who chills. And eats.

Johnny N.
Age 10

The Sunset

So this is what happened for one year for my 8th birthday. I went to Disney for my 8th birthday. And my family got to go to the beach after we left, and we had a good time. And when we look at the sunset, I tried to take a photo, but my phone? It died, and we went back home.

Johnny N.
Age 10

One day my mom said I had to try something new. So I told her *Can I play the games?* And she said, *You can try.* Something she told me to try was Basketball. I tried Basketball. Mom told me to try soccer. I tried Soccer. I tried Baseball. Then I tried Football. At first it wasn't fun because we had to run, jump, and do all this hard stuff. But after the first game it was so fun because we got to wrestle and drink Gatorade. I played defense and lineman. I still play football to this day.

Kaylin J-R
Age 9

Me and My Songs

I like TikTok songs because I get to learn the dance with my mom and my nana. And I also like TikTok songs because I get to post it with my family. I also like TikTok songs because I like playing it on Youtube on the TV and watching people dance. I love Rockstar by Polo G.— all you do is move your lips.

Kemari M.
Age 9

I Am From

From mom, grandma, my cousins, and my stepsister
From playing hot lava - my sister pushed me off the bed
From a bouncy castle at my uncle's birthday party
From food, my mom made
pasta with shrimp and broccoli

Kemari M.
Age 9

Everything is Gold

I love gold
I love my gold lion necklace
It has a jewel in its mouth
It's long
The whole thing is gold
His eyes is gold
His teeth is gold
His hair is gold
His head is gold
My uncle gave it to me for Christmas
About 3 years ago
I think I lost the bracelet
I love when my necklace is curled up
And round like an egg

Kevin M.
  Age 10

Love

I love my mom. I love how she tries to make it
  so we can pay bills.
  I love my dog because he comes to me.
  I love to play outside.
  The kids come and play and not be on
  phones, PlayStation, Xbox, and everything
  like that.
  I love how we play Uno.
  I love my family.
  I love my dad because he plays with me a lot
  We go to my dad's hometown on my
  brother's birthday.

Kevin M.
  Age 10
  The Day My Dog Came Home

It was 2020—the worst year ever—and we were all in quarantine. It
was June 2nd and we went to the dog shelter. In there was four dogs.
The first one was $100. It was a dog named Jose, we got him but we
had to wait for weeks. Weeks passed then we got him. He was so
happy he did "Zoomies"—that's what we call it; that's what we call
it when he is happy. His tail wags, then he gets his legs power, and
then he runs. This dog is something else. My dog is the dog, Flash.
My dog is sooooooo smart. One day me and Drew forgot to feed
him because we were new to this. So he grabbed his package of
food. Then we feed him 2 days later. Me and Jose watched.

Kidane G.
  Age 10

I Come From

I am from 4 sisters
  Sammir, Rahma, Rahel, Monica.
  My mom calls us by numbers.
  I am from Ethiopia— My dad had to
  walk a long way to the river for
  water and then walk back.
  At my old house we had a
  creepy Elmo doll that moved by
  itself. It jumped on my sister's
  head and tried to attack her.
  We moved.
  I play Fortnite, Roblox, and Minecraft.
  Roblox is a game with
  games inside of the game.
  There's Tower Battle
  and Tower Defense Simulator.

King F.
  Age 10

Roar

My mom is my trickster because when I was a little kid, I went to
my mom's room to ask her something and then a big sound came
from up there. So I still went upstairs and then I opened the door.
She wasn't there so I looked and a roar came from the back of the
door. I got scared, and she started to laugh and come from the back
of the door. I said *That's not funny*! And she gave me a hug. I was
kinda still scared and my godmother came and said *Hi*.

King F.
Age 10

Things I Love

I love going to Florida because Grandma
    lives in Florida
    I go there on my birthday
    And I love art because Anime
    If I never watched it I would not be drawing
    and going to art school instead
    My favorite Anime is Naruto
    I like it because it's about him having a spirit

Kori S.
Age 10

The Crazy One

My grandma, she pretends the TV is off and she more than once unplugged the TV. Now she put the dog in a new box and kick it down the stairs. I run to the stairs, and I fell on the floor and it hurt. So I look in the box and it's a stuffed animal. I had some ice cream and it helped me feel better.

Kori S.
Age 10

I Love

I love my bed
    I love my mom, she funny,
    she make me laugh
    I love my PS5 it's white
    I love Madden 21
    I love Boxing

I love See-food
   I love One Piece Manga
   I love XXX
   I love Ski Mask The Slump God
   I love Pop Smoke
   I love tattoos, I am gonna get a cross,
   my mom
   gonna get a goat and a butterfly

Manny O.
   Age 9

I'm From

I'm from Indianapolis
   I'm from Indiana and my mom
   Likes to cook for me and take care
   Of me.
   Noodles and last week she made
   Rice and chicken.
   And she takes care of me when I
   Was a baby.
   I like to do things with my family.
   To go out to eat.
   All of my family,.
   My aunts, my uncles, my Tio's
   My aunt takes me here.
   She always takes me to Legoland
   And to Chicago.
   I like to play football.
   I like my classroom and my teacher
   That's right here.
   And my teacher is the best teacher in
   The whole world
   And I never had the best teacher.

Manny O.
  Age 9

The Test

Last Friday or Monday I pass the swimming test. I had to swimming 1 feet 2 times. It was big, blue, and deep. I am very proud of myself.

Micah J.
  Age 9

I Am From

I am from Indiana
  Next to a school
  Next to my grandma's house

I come from a place
  Where we play games
  Xbox, my sister plays Fortnite

Every single day he works
  On Saturdays I come
  It's no joke

He wakes up at 3 in the morning
  He stays home Saturdays
  And plays games with us
  Mom watches random shows

Micah J.
Age 9

What I Love

My favorite dog is a Weiner dog. I was delivering a box with my dad. It was not a very long one, it was a happy dog. Maybe I'll get one if they do allow dogs when we move. I love having a place to stay at the hotel but that's all I like about it. Once we move it will be much better. I just want to be in a Sweet Potato Town. My dad has a secret recipe for Sweet Potato Pie. One hint: You need sweet potatoes. My favorite pie is Sweet Potato. I love my dad and my mom. My mom makes phone calls all day and sometimes watches TV. Then she makes lunch and picks us up. Sometimes my dad comes and picks us up. My dad works really hard. He delivers hundreds of boxes.

Neko W.
Age 10

The Time My Uncle Made Me Look Like A Lemon Head

I was at my uncle's house. I was taking a nap and I woke up and then I went to the bathroom and I looked into the mirror and MY HEAD LOOKED LIKE A LEMON!!! He had put mustard on my face. I was very mad, but at the same time it was very funny. And I am still planning how I am going to get him back to this day.

Neko W.
Age 10

The Day I Passed the Swim Test

When I got to the JCC, I was really nervous about doing my swim test. On the first swim day, I had to wear a life jacket, I really didn't care. On the second day, I tried my best and made it to 9 ft, but I still had to wear the life jacket because you had to make it to 11 ft.

Then, on the next swim day, I was so scared about the swim test, because I didn't want to wear the life jacket anymore. I really didn't pay attention, but I kept my eyes on Miss V. and just let myself glide and paddled very hard. I looked up and realized I was in the 11 feet. I was so happy! Then I had to float on my back for 30 seconds, I just leaned back and relaxed with my chest up. Finally, I got to go outside to the lazy river. I felt very proud.

Prunelle M.
Age 9

Terrible Pink

I got these new pink shoes for my birthday, I could not wait for school so I can wear them. School came by, it was raining, there was rain everywhere. I stepped in a puddle, then the shoes looked dirty. And my socks were wet and I had to wear them all day.

Prunelle M.
Age 9

I Come From

I am from indiana
I am from the sunset color I am
From the Bible I am from

Jazz I am from spaghetti
Because I love spaghetti
I am from Idolias
Because they are a beautiful and
Bright colors

Ramel G.
   Age 9

Pranking Sister

My sister is a very good pranking me, my brother, and my big brother and sister. She is good at pranking because she throws water on me. It made me mad, but I got her back by scaring her by jumping out of the closet. And got back at her again. I throw water on her.

Ramel G.
   Age 9

I'm From

I am from Indianapolis
I celebrate
Birthday with cookie cake
And ice cream cake
On the 4th of July
I go crazy
I like a lot of fireworks
I like bottle rockets

Ritchie C.
Age 9

The Most Beautiful Place

On my drive to Nashville, Tennessee I was very bored. It was still Winter, every two hours some snow would somehow fall on the windshield. Since Tennessee is in the South, it's warmer than it is over here. When I was halfway, I saw the most beautiful thing. The sun.

The sun was out and the snow on the trees sparkled. My sister said it looked like Narnia.

Ritchie C.
Age 9

Where I'm From

I'm from the Elf on the Irvington sign
    I'm from the pitbull named Princess
    Who barks.
    I'm from the dirty puddle
    Of tadpoles in my backyard.
    I'm from the tortas I ate.
    I'm from rap.
    I'm also from baseball.
    But mostly I'm from Irvington,
    Indiana.

Ritchie C.
   Age 9

The Hardest Thing I've Ever Done.

The hardest thing I've ever done was let go of my turtle. His name was Ralph, he was a box turtle. Believe it or not, he didn't like water. I love turtles. They're the best. I don't have a good history with pets. I had a dog named Rhino. I don't want to get into details with him. I had a dog named Scooby Doo and he was the best. I played Ninja Turtles with him!

Now back to the turtle. It was funny how he did pull ups. He would hook his claws onto the couch and pull himself up. We would let him out of his cage so we could feed him worms. There was mulch in his cage and the worms would just go into the mulch. He also ate crickets, raspberries, salad, and strawberries. I had him for a year and a quarter.

Rosie C.
   Age 10

A Trickster

The trickster in my life is my older brother Romeo. He is the trickster because one day I woke up after watching a scary movie the night before. I went to the bathroom to brush my teeth and then I went to the living room to find both my brothers sleeping on the couch. Romeo was sleeping peacefully. My little brother was snoring very loudly. Then I noticed someone drew a mustache and goatee with bright orange sharpie.

I tried to wake him up to tell him but he is a very heavy sleeper. So I took a picture instead. I went back to the bathroom then I looked in the mirror and I saw the humongous word *Loser* on my forehead. Then I knew— Romeo.

He drew on me and my little brother. He drew on me. Even worse, I had a unibrow, a beard, a long mustache. So I started planning how to get him back. Then I remembered that viral prank where you put their fingers in cold water and they start peeing their pants so I decided to try it. I was so mad at him I dunked his entire hand in and really quick he started to pee and I was satisfied. But for another quick laugh, I outlined my little brother's mustache and goatee with shaving cream. So with that story, I'd say me and my brothers are tricksters.

Rosie C.
    Age 10

The House With White Shutters

I am from a house with white shutters
    A metal door behind it a
    Forest in the forest
    A tadpole infested pond
    Beyond the forest a wide field
    With fallen trees
    Which gives me an eerie
    Chill beside the field an
    Abandoned train track at
    The house with the white shutters
    A dead end with
    A trail that leads to every backyard
    I am from the house with the white shutters
    Filled with four people

Rosie C.
　Age 10

The Secret Beach

Me and my family were hiking at Turtle Run. It was getting dark and I was drenched in water from a puddle I fell in earlier and I was very mad. I had little twigs in my hair. We were walking on a steep hill surrounded by bushes. I tripped over the fallen tree my family had already finished climbing over.

I fell into the bushes and was stuck in them for what seemed like 30 minutes. I crawled out, my clothes torn from the bushes. Then I saw it.

It was a little beach hidden from the trail. I laid down, forgetting I had just fallen 7 feet into bushes. I saw the sunset reflecting on the water. It was quiet. I would have stayed there all night but then I realized my family was probably already at the car.

I climbed up to find my brother looking for his shoe which he had lost in the mud. My family asked me where I was but I told them nothing about the beach 'cause it was my little beach.

Shaniyah J.
　Age 9

The Dog in the Trunk

One day or should I say noon or maybe afternoon I went over to my dad's house to spend time with him. The phone rang, *riing riing riing.* I would've answered it, but his ringtone, I don't remember what it sounded like. Turns out it was my mom calling saying *Can you go to the store and get Shaniya a mini book bag for her classes?* She said in a tiresome voice like she was asleep but she was not asleep she was... half sleep.

After she hung up, we got in the car and drove to Walmart or Target, one of those stores. We got a Hogwarts backpack, then we went to the car. He told me there was a..... puppy in the trunk. When we opened it? Turns out there was no puppy. It was actually a Hoverboard. It was pink and he gave me a helmet, knee pads, shock pads. I was so happy but I was kinda disappointed there was no puppy.

But after that it was time to go home. So we went back to the house and I played with Bella the dog and spent a little more time with my dad until my stepdad came to pick me up to go home with my new Hoverboard.

Shaniyah J.
   Age 9

I Am From

I am from
   No beaches
   No volcanoes
   My favorite place to go
   Is on vacations
   Like to
   Florida, Pennsylvania, Tennessee

Shazma M.
   Age 9

The Zoo

A beautiful place I have been was the Butterfly garden. I enjoy looking at the beautiful colors of the butterflies. And the fish were colored orange or orange and white. I was hoping one of the butterflies would land on me but they did not. We spotted a Butterfly that we had seen on Google— it looked like the top half of an owl!

I was scared when we were on the bridge upstairs 'cause I feel like the bridge will break. Me and my family went there together. We went there because of my mom's school. She worked and they were celebrating all the teachers that had passed the exam.

We went to the front where my mom's friends were, which are teachers, and they gave us tickets to get food, but I think they were coupons. We went to get membership. We looked at seals and sharks. I got to touch the sharks and stingray, then we looked at fish, a dolphin show, and ate food.

Shazma M.
   Age 9

I Am From

I am from Pakistan. I love the hot Halem. I am also Muslim. I also love eating Nihari and while we start waiting for the time of our Eid I couldn't wait to eat Chicken Pakora, Chicken Samosa, Rosa. I love it much more than the food I described. As Eid comes to an end, we get ready.

We wear Hijabs and dresses. My mom puts on makeup, her Hijab, and a nice dress. There are separate places. Men are in the front and women are in the back. The man on the microphone speaks words that I don't know, and then he starts speaking English only cause he's asking us something that does not always happen. He talks about Allah and at the middle, I get a comment from my brother, *Do you want candy?* he says. I say to get four bags. At the end, my dad tells me that Eid is a fun day for kids.

Syria W.
    Age 9

I Come From

I come from
    Hot and cold
    Sun up then down
    My grandparents are from Texas
    a sandy desert
    Crunchies fried chicken and creamy
    Mac and cheese friend of Earth
    Moist soil
    Reddish orange hair that's my aunt
    She makes the best food
    I grew up in a red brown house with bricks
    With a big grassy lawn.

Syria W.
    Age 9

What I Love in My Life

I love nature, the trees are high in the sky
    Bushes low on the ground in the soil
    I am the roots strong and bright

I love my mom's cooking
    She makes my favorite food mac and cheese
    It's cheesy and creamy

I love art
    Abstract
    A blast of paint splattered on a canvas

Trinity D.
Age 9

Ayyyy

I was at home listening to music when Rihanna came on. I got so hyped I got up and started dancing and my mom joined me. I said *Ayyyy* when I was dancing and I got dizzy. I saw the room was spinning. My mom asked if I was okay because my eyes were spinning. I said *Yes but I need some water*. She gave me the water and told me to take Tylenol. I said I still have a headache. My mom said you should probably lay down a few hours. Later I felt better. My mom said *Do you feel better?*

I said *Yes*.

Trinity D.
Age 9

The Whipped Cream Story

A trickster in my life is my sister and brother. It was a February night when I was sleeping and my sister and brother was awake so they poured water on me. It wasn't a lot, just a little. They poured it freezing cold and it was the middle of WINTER. The heat wasn't on and I had to sleep with cold clothes on. I had just got out the shower when they poured it. At first I did not feel it because it hadn't went through my clothes, but when I felt it, I woke up and had a mad look on my face.

They thought it was all funny games until I got them back. I each put whipped cream on their hand and tickled their nose and make them smack each other. So they started getting mad, and they never spoke to each other again that day. The next day they STILL were acting funny so I said *Y'all can cut it out now. It's just a prank!* They both gave me the death stare. I ran for my LIFE. So I already knew they were gonna get me back so I never went to sleep unless they did first. They never messed with me again..well, until a month later.

Tylan H.
Age 10

The Many Things I Love

I love to travel places.
I love that me and my family go someplace different every year.
I love going to expensive restaurants.
I love to go swimming and drift across the water.
I love to go to hotels.

I love watching Anime alone in my room. I love to eat Sushi.
I also love to play with my baby brother.
I love going to visit my cousins in Arizona.
I love that I get to see my dad after one week.

These are all the things I love. But one last thing I love is getting ice cream.
My favorite flavor is strawberry cheesecake,
because it is one of the best things I've tasted in my life.
I love the Grand Lux Cafe, because it is my favorite restaurant.

Tylan H.
Age 10

Pure Golden

Nine months ago I went to downtown Chicago. It was around 1 pm, and we were looking for a place to go for breakfast. Usually in downtown Chicago, you won't really see any restaurants except there are many Starbucks. We got in our car and then we saw a beautiful restaurant, it was a 2-story. I was amazed! I have never seen a 2-story restaurant. It would be an hour wait because it looked like business was booming, and the restaurant was packed.

When I finally got there, we saw doors that you would see in your average Hilton Hotel. As we rushed into the door, I was surprised by how many details there were! Signs on the wall and there were even escalators instead of a line of stairs. Since my baby brother was in a stroller, we went to take the elevator and the elevator was pure golden. And when I went to the biggest table I could find and when I turned my seat, I saw a big place where there were chefs all cooking the food! The food was amazing, and I will be sure to go back to Grand Lux Cafe again!

Valentino W.
    Age 9

Who I Am

I get to watch a lot of scary movies,
    Too much to count.
    I live in a peach house in the city,
    It is slow and busy.
    Sometimes, in my peach house,
    I play my favorite game.
    It's called Minecraft. I want to
    Play with my friends.
    I am from Indianapolis.

Valentino W.
   Age 9

The Day We Almost Drowned

We were at camp and we went on the bus and went to the JCC.
After that we went up and went to the pool to take the swim test.
Then we drowned.

I kept on floating. We had to float for 30 seconds. I floated for 25
seconds then started to drown. It did not feel good at all. I got lots
of water up my nose. I still want to go to the pool.

We take the test again on Friday. I might die.

Zaniyah C.
   Age 10

The Prank

One time when I was downstairs, my little cousin was coming down-
stairs, and I stood around the corner. I tried to hold in my laugh. I
was able to hold in my laugh until my cousin came down. When
they finally came down, my cousin almost fell on the floor. After I
scared my cousin, I was dying laughing and I almost fell on the floor
too. Then she pushed me on the floor because she was mad that I
scared her.

Then my other cousin was coming down the stairs. Once he came
down, we scared him. All he did was jump a little. I was still
laughing so everybody started laughing as well. Then we all went
upstairs and I acted like I "forgot" something. So I went back down-
stairs, turned the lights off, then waited for them to come downstairs
so I could scare them again!

A couple minutes later they came down and I scared them with the lights off. But this time they were really scared because they couldn't see a thing. I ran upstairs so I could pretend that I was upstairs the whole time. My cousins went to turn the lights on and I wasn't down there. Then they both came upstairs and saw that I was on the couch.

They came and asked if I was downstairs and if I scared them. I answered, *No.* They were both scared and thought it was a ghost that scared them. I was dying laughing and they was like, *Why you laughing???* I told them that I was downstairs and that I ran upstairs when they wasn't looking. They started not to believe me, but then they realized that ghosts were not real. Then they started laughing with me.

The End

Zaniyah C.
    Age 10

Honey, I Love

I love to go to Urban Air with my cousin.
    My cousin's name is Eliseyah.
    It is very fun to go with her because,
    She always lights up the mood.

I also love to go to Texas,
    Sometimes with my family.
    I go with my mom, dad, and little brother.
    His name is Tre.
    Tre is one-year-old.

My favorite store is Rue21.
    I go with my mom and sometimes my dad.
    I get hoodies and jeans.

I don't have a lot of hoodies, and
It is really cold in my new house.
And honey, I LOVE to do all of this stuff.

And honey I love you

The End.

Zyon P.
  Age 9

My Mom

I like the song "Amazing Grace" because it makes me think about my mom. Because it makes me feel how amazing she was before she died, happy and a little sad. My mom made the best spaghetti. My mom is the best mom in my life. I am grateful that she protected me. My mom is the best cook in the family. My mom won the award the first time for the police officer star of the week. I will always love and be grateful for my mom.

Zyon P.
  Age 9

Where I'm From

I am from smooth jazz.
  It makes me feel like a musician because
  I really like music.
  I also really like Country music,
  Because it make me feel like I
  Am on the prairie.
  I also like pizza,
  Gumbo,
  Cheeseburgers, and hot dogs,
  Because it is my favorite food.

We Are From

Camari, Kori, Miss Emily, Prunelle, Ramel, Ritchie, Rosie, Shazma, Syria, and Zyon

I am from smooth jazz.
    I am from North Carolina.
    I am from Texas.
    I am from Pakistan.
    I am from Indianapolis.
    I am from a house with white shutters.
    It's still burned in my brain.

I'm from sunset colors
    And new pink shoes.
    I hoped one of the butterflies would land on me but it didn't.
    On the 4th of July, I go crazy.
    Reddish brown hair - that's my aunt. She makes the best food.
    My mom made the best spaghetti.
    It's still burned in my brain.

The snow sparkled.
    My sister said it looked like Narnia.
    Maybe, just maybe, God will come around.

Saint Florian Youth Leadership Development Center

"That's where you want to be. It's an amazing program." These are among the first things many interns with the Indiana Writer's Center's summer Building a Rainbow program hear about Saint Florian. It's the big leagues. The name Firefighter Tony floats in and out of these conversations, along with familiar names of counselors and campers, many of whom have grown up and grown with Saint Florian, all the while sharing their stories with us.

Saint Florian is the patron saint of firefighters, so it is only right that he should also be the namesake of this program. At the Saint Florian Youth Leadership and Development Center, students learn, grow, do, lead, and think. Battalion Chief Firefighter Tony Williamson and the team of firefighters, counselors, drivers, teachers, donors, and volunteers have kept this program going because they believe in it. They believe in the power of leadership, entrepreneurship, teamwork, responsibility, and truth-telling. They believe in these kids who will become the next generation of leaders in Indianapolis and beyond.

The Saint Florian Center has been serving and uplifting Indianapolis youth for nearly thirty years, and the Indiana Writer's Center has been proudly partnering in this pursuit for eleven of those years. JC and CORE—our littles and middles—are where it all begins. Each group brings its own unique personality, changing year-to-year as the rotating cast of characters join us for the first time, age up, age out, and come into their own as young people.

We repeat this often because we believe it: it is an honor to be trusted with somebody else's story. We at the Writer's Center thank you, Saint Florian, for trusting us with yours.

JC, thank you for picking up your pencils, or handing them off to us when you need to.

CORE, thank you for allowing us to bear witness to your ever-changing voices and your ever-brightening minds.

We are honored. Instructors Miss Lyn and Miss Devon, Miss Barb and Miss Celeste, lead intern Miss Nykasia, and all of our newly-blossoming interns feel privileged and humbled to help usher your stories from your heads, your hearts, and your guts onto the page and out into the world to be heard.

If 2020 and 2021 have taught us anything, it's that we cannot know what is coming next. But it has also shown us, and we have shown ourselves, that we can do hard things. **You** can do hard things. The big hard things: viruses, violence, loss, isolation, and healing. The small hard things: spelling, speaking out loud, writing under a hot sun as the noise of the world carries on around us. Saint Florian, if you can do these things—and we know you can—and come out on the other side with your head held high, there is nothing you cannot do.

So, although we can't say for sure what the future holds, we know what you can do with it. We hope and pray to join you again next year, and many years beyond, to keep listening and learning and telling. Until then, keep changing the world. We can't wait to see you do it.

Devon Lejman
   Co-Instructor

Saint Florian Junior Cadets

———

Andres P.
    Age 7

Adult Fiction

I get up; I drink coffee.
    I drink coffee again.
    Then I go to work.
    Then I drink coffee.
    Then I drink coffee again.
    Then I go home.
    Then I drink coffee.
    Then I take a shower.
    And I drink coffee in
    the shower.
    Then I drink coffee
    again.
    Then I go to bed.

Andres P.
Age 7

I Love Dinosaurs

I know a lot of dinosaur names. More than I can keep track of. I can't even count! My favorite dinosaur is... ALL OF THEM! I learned about dinosaurs when I was 5 from books, TV shows, and my brain.

Some dinosaurs made it out alive from a volcano, but then more disasters happened. Dinosaurs used to run the world! If I met a dinosaur, I would say, "Hi, do you want to be friends?"

I feel smart when I talk about dinosaurs. People can learn from me. I'm teaching my mom about dinosaurs and when my baby sister grows up, I'll teach her too. I have a lot in common with dinosaurs!
Here is a list of dinosaur names:

1. Allosaurus
2. Velociraptor
3. T-Rex
4. Brontosaurus
5. Triceratops
6. Pterodactyl
7. Stegosaurus
8. Ankylosaurus
9. Brachiosaurus
10. Apatosaurus
11. Diplodors
12. Utahraptor
13. Arceaactix

Andres P.
    Age 7

Baby Sister

When I was the only kid in the house, I asked my mom if I could have a baby sister, and she said, *Yes!* When I was waiting for my baby sister, I waited at my grandpa's house for 3 days. When she was born and when I first saw her, I was as happy as a kid in a candy store. Her name is Ari.

When she got older, I played with her a lot. One time I taught Ari how to say the ABC's, but she did not get it very well. She can say *Mommy*, *Daddy*, and *Yes* and *No*. As she got older, she started to walk. I was so proud of her. She can climb up the stairs, but she can't get down yet.

She chases me a lot. We play tag, and we get tired a lot. One time we had a dance battle, I think I won. I wanted to trash talk, but I couldn't because she is a baby. When she turned 1, we went to our dad's house, and we played. We bought a giant balloon that said *It's fun to be one!* We found popsicles at the store, and they were cool because they said *firecracker*. I thought it would be a cracker on fire because it was in a freezer, but it wasn't.

Antoine B.
    Age 8

My Day

Help people at the shelter.
Help people on the streets.
Buy stuff for people, like homeless people.
Buy food for babies.
Buy food for grown-ups.
Watch TV and play my games.

Watch movies.
Have my family over for a party.
Pet my dog and play with it.
Go swimming.
And that's it!

Antoine B.
   Age 8

My Friends and My Dog

I met my friends Gary and Josiah at camp. Gary is my favorite friend. He likes to play around. We play tag and basketball. Gary wears a black Marvel hat and he has braids. He wears a toy watch. Josiah has braids, too. He has a dog and a swimming pool. I go to his house. Sometimes I play with his puppy. It doesn't have a name yet.

I had a dog. My dog was named Diamond, she died in a storm. She was white, and she was brown. And she had little puppies. She acted nice. If there were people she didn't know, she'd bark at them. I would play fetch with her and sometimes I would put her in my toy car when she was little.

Blair A.
   Age 8

King's Island

I drowned in the Waves Pool. Big waves too. I was swimming and I went to the Big Slide.

I took a break and then went back on the slide and went very fast. My cousin was with me; we weren't scared. I was scared the first time but not anymore. I went on it 5 times. My cousin and I went down together. I went down the orange one. He went down the blue one.

Blair A.

Age 8

My Friend Hailey

Once I spent a time with a girl named Hailey. She was nice and pretty and funny. She was my friend. She helped me write and read about flowers and strawberries and brown leaves and yellow soft hair and pink glasses and black pants and a striped white and black shirt and a black mask. She has kindness. She is in the reading center. Hailey: Black boots, lots of earrings, green and white socks, a blue moon star case, a blue phone. She smells like Starbucks.

Bryce D.

Age 6

I Like Staying at My Grandmas

I want to stay home because I'll go to my grandma's house and play games and spend time with my grandma. My sister and I play tag. We start laughing when I fall down. I'll eat Takis and my sister eats them too. I play WWE with DJ and Chris. Chris gets mad because we do teams. Last time? I threw him up in the air and caught him! We win big matches and the fire at the entrance will light up.

Bryce D.

Age 6

M&M Cookie Joy

Since you asked I will tell you why I am happy. I am happy because I love M&M cookies. We buy them from the store and take them home. When we get home I eat three at one time. Then when I get done, I go to bed.

Cadence D.
Age 7

What Makes Me Black and Proud

What makes me proud about me is when I get my hair straight, you can see my long hair and when it gets wet, it curls back up, and when it gets hot, it does the same thing. And sometimes I get braids, and when you go in the pool and when you have braids, it is a less harder time to wash it out. And when you do not have braids, it is harder to wash out. And when you have straight hair, it is not that hard, because it takes them like 5 or 10 minutes and that is why I like being Black, my hair.

Cadence D.
Age 7

My Baby Sister

This story is about my mom and my baby sister. My mom has black hair curly hair and is pretty, nice, loving, caring. Me and my mom go to different states together, and we always go to the park, states, and the pool. And I love her so much! And we go shopping together, and she is so brave, fun, loving, and caring.

So, now this is what happened before my baby sister was born. So I think we took my mom to the hospital. And the baby came, and my mom named her Aria. And we stayed in the hospital and after a few days later, she got to come home.

And next year she turned 1, and she had a bounce house and a big one for her party theme. And there was a watermelon theme, and she had these fruits and candy on it. It was so fun! Our family was there, and it was super fun.

And for her first Christmas, we got an Xbox and these cool chairs, some body stuff, new toys, new electronics, new games. And my baby sister got a new dress and some new toys. and a LOL doll. I got new pants, new shirts, boots, new PJs and we ate some gingerbread cookies, and we had some Christmas dinner. That's the end of that story

And then she turned 2. That birthday was animal themed, and she had a DJ and we ran stuff. It was so fun, and she had some good snacks!

Carson S.
Age 8

Let me Tell You About COVID-19

Jeffrey does not know about Covid-19 so let me tell you about it. It kills so many people. It closed the zoo and the movie theater and school. I had to learn online. We had to Zoom.
BUT!
I like learning online.
I don't want to go to back to school.
I like being at home.
I want to stay away from kids I don't know.
I want to stay away from the bad kids.
Love, Carson

Carson S.
Age 8

A Shout Out to My Mom
Number 1: I Ignored Them

The first day of school people were being mean to me, and I just ignored them because I knew it was gonna happen. Then the next day I tried to make some friends, but they were being mean to me so I ignored them.

I tried again and again. I told my mom, and she said be cool and act like them and calm down. The third day I went to school I did what my mom said and I acted cool and calmed down. And I made some friends and I had to thank my mom so much.

Number 2: I Got Lost

I got lost in the store. I was with my mom, and I wanted something. I went to go to my mom, but she wasn't there. I ran around, and I found my mom. I was so scared, and I was sad that I would never see my mom again.

Number 3: The Hardest thing

I was watching TV. My mom told me to get in the car; we were going to get the storage. Me, my Brother, and my mom were carrying heavy boxes.

I was like, "Mom these are heavy! Really heavy!"

I had no choice. I HAD to do it. We put all the boxes in the storage; we went home; I got on YouTube and took a nap too. The next day, we went to the storage again, I was still sleepy, but I had to go carry heavy boxes, still sleepy.

Again, I was exhausted, so I waited in the car. I was very sleepy and fell asleep; we went home; I fell back to sleep.

All of this heavy lifting was tiring me out. I couldn't take it anymore! But, my mom, my brother and me were moving. I was like, *Stay awake until you get home, Carson.*

And I did. It was worth it, so we could move.

Cayden B.
Age 6

The Sad Lost Dog

My TT lost her dog. He was named Tiger. He had brown fur and was a little bit big. He chased me around. He was not that friendly. He almost bit me! He barked loud, a big man bark. I threw the ball for him, and he brought it back. My godfather, Brandon, was very sad when Tiger died. He cried. I feel sad when he died. I was also scared that he would turn into a zombie dog!

Cayden B.
Age 6

Lucas Oil and Monster Truck

The football stadium is Lucas Oil Stadium in the city. I went there for the monster truck show. The trucks had lots of detail. Some had fins, some had dog ears, some had zombie arms. The zombie one made lots of smoke, some cars were blue, purple, and yellow. They sounded like "rar rar rarrrgh!". I went with my mommy. I had a cheeseburger and a hot dog. My favorite was Megladom. It got first place two times! I cheered. When I got home I watched YouTube.

The end.

Charles M.
Age 6

Dear Martin Luther King,

I like my skin color, because it is so cool, and it's so powerful. I learned that my own self. My sister's skin color is powerful too.

And I wanted to let you know that I always have to keep my dinosaur mask on when I go out roller skating, swimming, or to the grocery store.

Goodbye!
    Charles

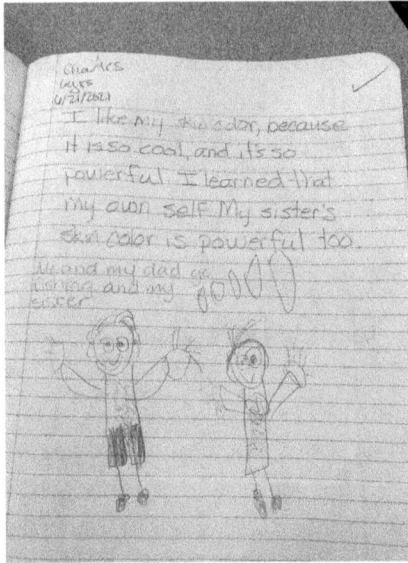

Christian S.
    Age 7

My Morning

I play on my iPad.
    I made a drink.
    I got ready for camp
    I got washed up.
    I put on my clothes.
    My Pop dropped me off.
    And the last thing, I helped other people at
    camp.

Christian S.
    Age 7

I Lost My Favorite Stuff

I lost my favorite slime ball.
    I lost venom ans Spiderman toy.
    I lost my password and phone.
    I lost my favorite shoes.
    I lost my favorite stuff.

JC Counselor Elyjah M.
    Age 16

What It Means to Be Black

I love Black people. Talented, funny, misunderstood individuals.

All over the world, there are Black people with limitless talent.

So much swag. So powerful.

I love my family, and when we gather together? So many laughs. So much love.

As long as I live, I will always believe that we are special in so many ways whether it be dancing, music, writing, singing Whatever it may be, we excel at it.

We're amazing. I love everything about Black folk.

JC Counselor Elyjah M.
　　Age 16

When I Felt Like My Black Life Didn't Matter

I've always excelled in my classes my whole life. I have. And I've always been the only Black boy in my class. That was, until middle school. I remember I had an Afro, and I brought my Afro pick to school.

My teacher took me to the principal's office, because I had a "weapon". The whole situation was blown way out of proportion. Now that I'm reminiscing on this day, I'm really disappointed in my teacher. Although I don't remember her name, I really wish I could ask her about her thought process.

All around disrespectful.

JC Counselor Elyjah M.
　　Age 16

2020/2021

2020-2021 was definitely... a year. A lot of the best, but also the worst you know? Many, many, many not-so-great things have occurred. But it's taught me many things.

Like, how to accept everything for what it is/who they are. 20/21 made me stronger than I've ever been. Helped me fully understand who I am, and the person I want to be. It's helped me communicate my feelings.

I hope nobody has to experience living through a pandemic where all the places we go and all the things that make us human... are closed. Where our beautiful faces are covered by a piece of cloth that restricts many from breathing the air we were made for breathing. The many things we do as human beings we were unable to do due to the pandemic.

JC Counselor Marquia T.
　　Age 19

Black Girl Joy

My hair will greet you before my mouth does. Waving a soft, yet energetic hello and goodbye. She encourages you to stand tall even on rainy days. She represented togetherness and teamwork as she coils one strand to another. Bouncing in shine. Shining in storms.

My eyes will read you before I meet you. Finding depth in your ways and tone. Drawing your character out in my world and finding you a role to play. Glistening with the stars and moon— living a fantasy out of imagine.

My tongue will challenge you. Words hitting like Tyson, leaving a sting like poison. My speech is unmatched. If I stutter, you heard me. I do not repeat myself. Move with my words like ocean tides.

My skin will protect me from the sun. I am of the sun carrying a bit of magic from the heavens. Melanin is her name, and she's worth more than your wedding band. Glimmering like gold, mocha like coffee. The darker the berry, the sweeter the juice. The darker the skin, the deeper the roots.

JC Counselor Marquia T.
Age 19

Things I Do

I drive barefoot.
I crack my knuckles probably thirty times a
day.
I watch my shows with subtitles.
I put my left sock on before my right one.
I step into my dresses instead of pulling it
over my head.
I sit my purse on the ground-- so unlady like.
I let my phone die all the way even when
sitting next to my charger.
I don't pull off without turning my music on.
I brush my teeth with coconut oil.
I see my face and body differently than
others.
I don't tie my shoes.
I wear crocs to any occasion.
I tell jokes to myself.
I run from the grease when I drop fries in the
skillet.
I massage oil into my skin.
I work daily.
I challenge my life and others.
I love with my whole heart.
I do.

JC Counselor Nia
Age 16

Being Black

Being Black is happiness. Celebrating our wins and success together as a community.

Being Black is sadness. Fearing for the well-being of our friends and family when situations arise. Being fearful of the police or how others perceive us due to our race.

Being Black is persistence and never giving up, despite having the odds being stacked against us.

Being Black is belonging to a beautiful, diverse community.

Being Black is a long standing tradition, music, and dancing.

Being Black is laughter and cookouts and family.

Being Black is supporting others.

Being Black is power and advocating for others.

Being Black is power and advocating for what is right.

Being Black is knowledge.

Being Black is setting trends.

Black is power.

Black is love.

JC Counselor Nia
   Age 16

Letter to my Future Self

Dear future me,

How are you?

What's the world like now?

Right now the world is pretty crazy. One of the hardest experiences of my life has been the past year. Due to Covid, there were a lot of things that changed in my life. I missed out on a family reunion in Florida, my entire sophomore year, and seeing friends and family. My mental health was awful. I couldn't bring myself to do homework, I always felt sad or stuck, and I didn't have any outlets for those feelings.

I missed football games and school dances. I missed going out with friends. Everyday felt the same as the one before on repeat. I was tired all the time and felt the pressure of getting older without any of the experience that people value in high school. The pandemic is still going on, and while most of my friends and family are vaccinated, it is still upsetting when events are cancelled.

I hope you're alright! I already know you're successful of course, but I wonder what you're doing.

Are you a psychologist?

A politician?

Where did you graduate from?

Did you move out of the country like you planned to?

I really hope you're happy.

Do you still have any of the same friends?

Where have you traveled?

Did your sense of style change? How much?

Where do you live?

How have your opinions changed?

How much money do you make?

How is the family? Oh no, does Caiden have kids? If so, how many times did he drop them?

Anyways, I hope you continue to be amazing and change the world for the better. There is no doubt in my mind that you are or will do amazing things!

Bye bestie, enjoy your night!

Devin F.
   Age 7

It's the Little Things

My friends make me angry when they fight.

My mom makes me sad when she cries.

When my mom and I go places, it makes me happy.

When my mom cheers for me in soccer and says, "You can do it!" I feel proud. And I make a goal!

Devin F.
Age 7

Traveling with my Mom

Me and my mom went to Arizona.
We went to the park.
We went to the Grand Canyon and then to
the water park.
Then we went to Texas!

Dylan I.
Age 8

Every Day

What I do every day is...I wake up and eat breakfast. Everyday, I brush my teeth and I put my clothes on. And after, I play on my game. Every day I have school, my mom helps me with my homework, after we spend time together.

Every day, I go to bed and after I wake up in the morning, I go to school.

When I get out of school, I go to my aunt's house and she helped me figure out what we did in school. She helped me figure out what to eat and then I went home and went to bed.

I went to school in the morning and then I went to my grandma's house. I played with my dog and watched a movie. After that I went home.

The next day I went to school and then to my friend Elijah's house. At his house we had a water gun fight and played indoor soccer. We watched a movie and then I spent the night, I ate breakfast and we played for a little bit. We went to a Halloween party and I got to hit a Pinata.

My mom came and when we went home we watched a movie.

Dylan I.
Age 8

Happy and Hard

The people that make me happy are my mom and my grandma and my pops. They make me happy because they talk to me. Eating spaghetti, my favorite food, makes me happy. And so does playing Sonic Motor Ultimate Game and Mortal Kombat II.

The hardest thing I had to learn how to do was swim. I was 6 or 7 years old, and I did swim lessons at the new YMCA. I was a little bit scared because I knew the water was cold, and I thought the water was going to be deep. When I jumped in the deep end, I thought I was going to sink. My swim instructor told me to stop struggling and stay calm. Then I started to float. I was happy.

Eli W.
Age 6

Tigers Are Scary

Tigers are scary. They can eat you, but guess what? When I'm with my uncle, I cannot get eaten because I'm with my uncle!

So I say, "Sweet dreams, Tiger." I say this when the tiger goes to sleep quietly. "Sweet dreams to you, Tigers." I will see you next year. I'm going to hang out with my uncle and stay the night for 3 nights. I'll see you later, Tigers!

Eli W.
Age 6

The Day
The Day Part 1: Like I'm 30

When I get up for the day, I eat some ice cream, I drink some water, I take a shower, and then I go to my job like I'm 30.

And then when it's bedtime, I brush my teeth, wash my face, and then I go to bed.

The Day Part 2: Beautiful Day

When the sun shines, it's morning, and the best day ever.

When it rains, I can't play. When it rains, I have to play inside. But, I'm always happy because it's a beautiful day.

Today is a happy day, and today's a good morning because it's shining bright. I wake my mommy up and then I go with my mommy to her job and then I probably will do some school work.

And also I love the world; it's the best! I will see Banner and Mr. Kevin later, and I will go to my house and watch TV, then have dinner and get ready for bed.

And then tomorrow is a whole new beautiful day.

Elijah A.
Age 8

The Things I Do and Think About

I wake up, get dressed, go to summer camp, play, and do stuff until 4:00 p.m. Then I play with my sis and then take a shower, then play with my friend Jeremiah, then go to sleep. But before that, I eat mac and cheese, chicken, Burger King or Rallys.

Slip, slip, slip, "OWWCH!" That's because I have a really slippery floor at home.

And then I think about all that die from smoking and cancer.

Elijah A.
Age 8

Tall Hair

My hair was tall.

And my mom, she— every time it grows back tall— she makes me cut it down. It makes me mad because my hair being tall makes me unique. But she say, "It grows back!"

I feel happy when I have tall hair, and when it grows back, I can get curls.

Gary M.
Age 9

Being Black

I didn't
choose
to Be Black:
I just got
lucky.

Gary M.
   Age 9

My Pets

I lost more than one pet, the first one was an American Bulldog named King. He played with me. He chased me. King was so strong he dragged my sister when he was on the leash.

One day he was playing in the grass and I picked up his bone— he bit me! He was only a puppy, but my mom sold him to my Nana and my Nana sold him, and I didn't see him anymore.

Then I had 2 small Chihuahuas, but my mom sold the black one named Prada. Chanel ran away, and we never found her. They tried to get in the pool. They knew how to swim and float. They made me laugh.

Now I have 2 cats named Panther and Sylvester. They play together. I miss playing with King.

Gregory A.
   Age 7

How I Got Lost

I am in the city, and I got lost, and I have to get back to my house. I didn't know where to go. I was walking on the sidewalk, so I don't get hurt in the road. I was with my brother. My mom and dad found me and packed me up in the car. After they found me, I went home.

Gregory A.
Age 7

Saint

Saint is following me to the zoo. And then he followed me to the museum. And he followed me to the art museum.

He's just like me. And he follows me at school too. He's in my grade. At my school grade, I get an S+ and Saint gets S++ because Saint knows what math is. He knows a lot of math.

We got extra recess.

He said, "You wanna go on the swings?" And I said "Yes!" And he followed me home because he's my friend.

Saint is a real person, born by the universe. He can live here or in space.

Ian H.
Age 9

The Hardest Thing I Had to Do

The hardest thing I had to go through was surgery. I had to get new cells and blood in my body because I have Sickle Cell. I still go to the doctor for checkups. My brother had to go through it twice. He went to Riley and St. Louis Children's Hospital. My mom is a nurse and helps out with neurosurgery. My dad is a pediatrician. They both work at Riley Children's Hospital.

Ian H.
 Age 9

My New Friend

My new friend; his name is Blair. He goes to Saint Florian and is sitting by me. We met at the beginning of camp. Both of us have gone for 2 years. Blair plays fortnight and soccer. He is the mayor which means he is our leader for our group.

Jada J.
 Age 8

I Fell So Crazy

The hardest thing I went through was falling off a motorcycle. I was on a kid motorcycle, and I was going so fast, like 100 miles per hour.

My grandma was behind me telling me to slow down, but I didn't hear her. When I was coming back to the house, I was going fast, and I almost fell in the grass and almost hit a light pole.

I broke my left leg and it hurt so bad. On a scale of 1 to 100, it hurt a 200! My leg and ankle were scraped and I couldn't walk. I haven't ridden the motorcycle since.

Jada J.
 Age 8

Black Skin

One day this kid named David said that my Black skin color was ugly. When he said that I was sad and mad, so I told the teacher. The teacher told him that he would get in trouble, but she forgot.

David said, "That's why the teacher forgot because your Black skin is ugly." So I told the teacher again and David got expelled, and I was happy.

I love my Black skin, because I don't have to wear makeup.

I love that my Black skin matches my hair color.

Jada J.
    Age 8

Little Mont

He died on my mom's birthday.

My brother.

He was 24.

Somebody shot him while he was inside his car. The person who shot him didn't go to jail because my brother's friend shot him. He died too.

My brother's friend drove my brother to the hospital, but my brother died on the operating table.

Sometimes when Momma leaves he, my other brother, my sister and me—he takes care of us. He fixes me noodles—ooh! And pancakes, bacon, and eggs.

What I miss most about him is that he played with me and bought me stuff like toys.

He was tall, good looking, with a real smile. His dad is Big Mont. He was Little Mont.

Javion W.
Age 9

My Daily Life

I do Livestream on Twitch for Minecraft.
I make TikTok videos.
I watch Youtube.
I ride my bike to McDonalds to get dinner.
I play with my 5 cats: Sylvester, Gibson,
Kitty, Snowball, and Marshmallow.

Javion W.
Age 9

Cats

This one time I was waiting for my package to come. Soon I found out that it was canceled. But I got 5 cats instead, and I was surprised!

My dad bought me the cats. They were small, but now they are big. The first cat had babies so now I have 7 cats! Only one of them likes tuna, and the other ones like cat nibble.

Josiah T.
Age 8

My First Day at School

One time I was at my first day of school, Lakeside Elementary School. I was in Kindergarten. My older brother said he was going to stay with me. But, he had to go to his class. My teacher was nice, and I was a good kid. My grades were always good, and I was never mean to anybody. And I had lots of friends. And soon, I had a girlfriend, Layla.

Josiah T.
   Age 8

Teacher

black hair
light colored skin
dressed nice
she liked Wonder Woman & ladybugs
Ms. Lauvre
sounded high & deep
classroom smelled nice

Josiah T.
   Age 8

Lost With A Skin of a Different Color

One day, it was about 3 months ago, me and my brother wanted to play basketball. My mom drove me there. We played for about 30 to 40 minutes, then we tried to go to the shortcut home, but the road was busy so we tried another way.

We went up to a store about 50-60 minutes later, and we found a lady. Her skin was a different color. I said "Excuse me," then she moved out of the way. I thought she was rude, then I said "Excuse me" again "Can you help me find my mom?" Then I started crying, tears running down.

Then she gave us her phone. My mom answered. She almost didn't answer the phone. About 10 to 20 minutes later, my mom came. I went running to her crying cuz I love my momma, and she let us buy anything we want. I got an awesome toy gun. It was used in a movie.

Then I got some candy and I had a bottle of Gatorade.

Kaiden S.
Age 9

My Black Boy Joy

I am going to tell you how I learned to appreciate my skin tone so sit back, relax, and enjoy this article.

To start things off, I was in the car, and we were getting out at Walmart, and I said I want to be white. Of course, my mom got mad. I was 6. so I did not know why she was mad.

Now, 3 years later, I am starting to understand.

Kaiden S.
Age 9

Future Child

Dear Future Child,

I am the person from the past. 2020 was one of the worst years ever. Coronavirus was so bad, that we had to do a quarantine aka a pandemic.

You are lucky now.

Love, Me

Layla W.
Age 9

Having a Hard Time

I got up for school and my mom told me I can not go to school. I was crying, cuz I did not get to go to school cuz my mom told me that my papa is not good, and he will not survive. I started crying.

Layla W.
    Age 9

Why I'm Happy

I am having a lot of fun.
I like to do activities.
I like to write.
I like math.
I like to go to the pool.
I like to do TikTok.
I like to make new friends.
I like to go to camp.
I like to eat Lay's.
I like getting my dog a cake for his birthday.
I'm happy.

Leana W.
    Age 7

Black Girl JOY

My family goes to the pool. We swim in the water. The water was warm. I like to eat burgers with my family and hot dogs and fries.

My friend Harmony and I play on the swings. We feel happy and like we are flying.

I love going to the mall too. I like to look at the clothes. When I get new clothes I feel happy.

When I first got my braids, my hair made me happy.

Leana W.
Age 7

My Grandpa and My Dad

When I was 6 years old, my grandpa passed away. He was 95 years old. When he was alive, my favorite thing to do with him was go to the dollar store. He would always buy me fidgets.

My grandpa also bought me a pink bike with a purple and pink tail. The best thing that he bought me was the Barbie Camper Power Wheel. It is pink and blue in the front. Me and my friend would always drive in the camper. We would put our Barbies in it and drive until it was time to stop and have a picnic.

I love my dad. He is nice. On my sixth birthday, he got me a blue bike. I was happy because me and my dad ride bikes. We ride our bikes to Walmart. When my bike broke, my dad fixed my bike. It made me happy; my dad is really nice to me.

Maddison S.
Age 9

My Black Joy

Im'a be talking about how I Love my black joy. I Love my black joy because I Love the way my hair goes in an afro when I go to the pool and how long my hair is.

And for the most part, I love how my skin glows through the hot sunny sun when it's summer. Some activities I like to do is cheerleading in my backyard and on my trampoline.

Maddison S.
Age 9

To the Future Babies

To all the Future Babies,

It's been a rough year last year with all the Covid-19 going around and celebrities dying and stuff.

And school was shutting down, and we had to go on Zoom instead of going to school. But in my opinion, I kinda liked Zoom instead of real school because we got to eat whatever, watch TV, and NOT DO HOMEWORK!

But I missed my friends sometimes. And with Covid-19, I had to move here so I really missed my friends.

But that's all.

Maddison S.
Age 9

My Glasses

I used to hate my glasses. It was my first time at my new school after I moved. So I walked into school with my glasses on— it was my first day. I was scared and embarrassed because I had no friends.

But then a girl named Isis come up and greeted me in the class, and I was not scared anymore cause I made a new friend and she noticed my glasses, and she said she liked them!

And I was happy for my new friend, and I love my glasses now. <3

Malaya M.
   Age 6

Talking About Feelings

What makes me happy is to go to the park and to go to camp. What makes me really happy is when we go to the water park. What also makes me happy is when I can eat candy.

I'm happy when I'm at the mall. I cry and am sad when I hurt myself. And I'm mad when my brother messes with me.

Malaya M.
   Age 6

My First Day of First Grade

I was scared on my first day of first grade. There were tables, cubbies, and shelves. There was a big screen and a big rug with a picture of North America and South America and Africa and Texas.

My teacher was nice. We was doing fun stuff like drawing and free time. I made friends. They were Skylar and Nia and Andrian and Emir. We played together and we got to do show and tell and we got to play with toys outside. When we got there, we got our seats at the table. They had our names on them. At the end of the day I felt happy.

Marcel M.
   Age 9

What Makes Me Mad

What makes me mad is when I get yelled at especially when I didn't do anything at all! And when bugs bite me and make me itchy.

That's not fair!

What else makes me mad is when really bad guys rob stores. It also makes me mad when people kill other people for no reason. It makes me mad when people drown and die. I get mad when people get kidnapped.

It makes me mad how some people be lying. It makes me mad when people are unfair.

It also makes me mad how people keep dying from Covid and the numbers keep going up.

Marcel M.
    Age 9

People That Help Me

The Indiana Writers Center helps me write stories. The stories are about what makes me feel emotional and what's the stuff I do in my life. The Indiana Writers Center helps me write when I don't know what to write. I like to think of stories, and I like when the Center helps me write them. I have people write things for me because my handwriting isn't so good. I have people write stories like this for me.

Other people who help me are my Coaches Wilsons. They are my track coaches who help me run faster. Coaches Wilsons. There are two of them Miss Wilson and Coach Wilson. They help me build up my speed. They also help me do the long jump. My favorite race is the 100 meter dash and the 4x100 relay dash. I'm good at both sprints and long distance. I do better at the distance. The 400 is one race I do really well at. Our team is called Benjamin Harrison YMCA Fliers.

The camp counselors and the firefighters at camp St. Florian also help me everyday. They keep me positive. They tell me when I get back to school, I can be a good kid and I can be a leader and be kind. I can make the world a better place!

Marcel M.
     Age 9

Daddy

My daddy surprised me when he came home from war. He was in the Army. He flew all the way out of America on an airplane. I felt happy when he came home.

I was watching a movie, and he came randomly in! At first I didn't recognize him. When I hugged him I asked, *Who is this?* Then I felt his face and realized there were holes in his face (my dad always picks his face). Then we hugged.

My dog named Tyson barked. We picked up my dog, Reese. She was so excited to see my dad.

One of my big brothers was in a different state, so he wasn't there to see him. My big brother was so happy that he almost cried. My little sister was so happy too. We all took a picture.

I appreciate my dad. He is still home today.

Michael H.
     Age 6

Play

First, I go to the park and I play monkey bars and then I play with the swings. I play with my sister Mikayle and after I play with my sister, we climb on the ropes and a big swing.

After the park, we go back to the house and ride bikes. Our mom also lets us do stuff without asking. Dinner is always good. What I eat is turkey, turkey wraps, mashed potatoes, and I drink water. For dessert, we eat strawberry ice cream, and my sister eats chocolate.

And then we go outside and camp outside, we get some marshmallows and make s'mores. We sleep outside in the tent. We go to bed at 3:30 in the morning. My favorite part of the day is going playing outside.

Michael H.
    Age 6

Black King

My mother and my father tell me I am a Black king, and I can do great things in life through Jesus Christ. My mom says one day I am going to grow up.

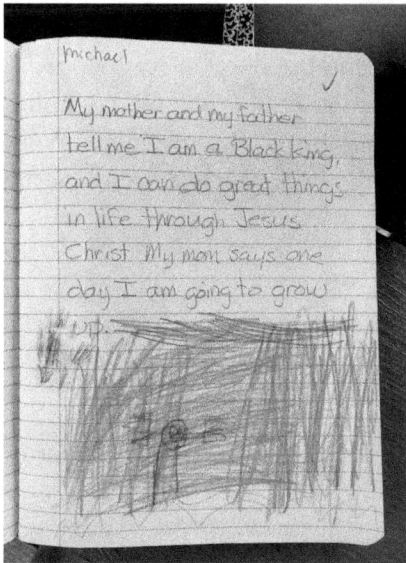

Michael H.
   Age 6

Brother

Once I lost my baby brother. He was on the street. Then he got hit by a car. It made me feel kind of nervous. The car was big. His arm was bleeding, but he didn't cry. He doesn't cry. He's a big boy sometimes. Actually, all the time.

Pheldon M. III
   Age 8

My Sister

My sister is very nice to me. She tickles me and she lets me get on her back. She's being nice to me because I'm being good. I'm 8; she's 17. She is 9 years older than me. Her name is Jalin.

When I ask her something, she'll say "Yea." But when she catches my little brother hitting the dog, he gets popped by Jalin. So I don't do what my brother does. She stole my dad's phone from me. I said "Give it back!" She started chasing me. I pulled it, but I wasn't strong enough to get it back. When I get it now, I hide it.

Pheldon M. III
   Age 8

Getting Spooked To Death

It was a nice day when I went into the aquarium. We went to a shark cage, and on the top it said *Touch at your own risk.*

So, I touched it and….nothing happened. Until a shark came charging at the window!

I slammed into another wall. I was so scared, and my cousins were like...

Oh my God, what happened? What happened?!

I got spooked to death!

Trinity W.
  Age 7

Zoom

I love Zoom because…

1. We don't have to go in person.
2. We get to lay in bed.
3. I get to eat home food. And it's soooo good!
4. I get to play with my dog at break time.
5. I get be at home.

I love being at home because...

1. At lunch I get to eat what I want. My mom sometimes makes me peanut butter and jelly.
2. When I'm done with school, I can play with my toys - like my brother's iPad.
3. I like to lay in my bed. It's so warm.

I didn't miss my friends very much.

Trinity W.
Age 7

Pops and Mom

I lost my Pops in *December*. When I was sick, he was funny and silly and made me feel better. I lost my dog a long time ago. She was a small Chihuahua.

I love my mom so much! On my birthday, she got me, she gave me *lots of money* for my birthday and my dad bought me a bike for my birthday. My mom is silly and funny. She makes me laugh. She tells silly jokes and makes funny faces. She is crazy! And she is pretty. Her hair is short and curly like mine. She likes to do TikToks with me.

Tsion M.
Age 7

My Black Girl Joy

MY BLACK GIRL
JOY
SHINES.
MY
SKIN
SHINES
SO BRIGHT AS
GOLD.

Tsion M.
   Age 7

My Locs

I love my locs because they are growing so fast and long. I want to take out my locs, but I can't because it will be too harsh on my hair.

My locs are too pretty and beautiful to take out. I can't wait until they get so long down my back, so I can put it in a ponytail or bun.

One time my hair stylist put my hair into two flower petals and for my birthday, she put them into two pigtails. I love all of the beautiful hairstyles that I can wear with my locs.

BLACK ROYALTY

Cadence D. 7, Tsion M. 7, Michael H. 6, Maddison S. 9, Jada J. 8, and Lead Intern Nykasia W.

I love my Black skin

I love the way it glows

Bright as GOLD

Black Kings

Black Queens

We are Royalty

And we shine as bright as GOLD

Melanated skin

Kinky, Curly hair

Small fro or Big fro

Locs or Twists

We are Royalty

And we shine as bright as GOLD

———

Adrian L.
Age 10

Dear Future Brother,

The year of 2020 was challenging and hard on everyone. There was no more toilet paper, and we had a lock down. We had to stay inside, and it was boring. There was a lot of curfews, and so many people died. It was so sad. We had so little toilet paper that every time we had to use the bathroom, you had to save.

I was sad because of all the people who were dying. I was sad because people's loved ones were dying because of the virus. But it's getting better, and we are learning how to handle this virus. The vaccine is very helpful and with the vaccine, this virus will be over with. The only thing that kept me from being bored is electronics and my phone and TikTok.

I look forward to a new world.

Love, Me

Adrian L.
Age 10

Black Boy Joy and Mother Joy

Today I am going to write about a time that someone made me feel sad and a time people judged me. I went to school and everyday there was something that people just didn't like about me.

One day it was, I'm too dark. But everyday, it was insult after insult. These insults made me feel bad about myself. But everyday someone had something mean to say about me. I wished everyday that people would stop talking about me. They were stealing my black boy joy. It made me feel bad about being black.

Until one day, I finally had the courage to talk to my mother. She was surprised and mad at me for not telling her sooner. But even though I was wrong for this that day, my mother taught me the most important life lesson ever in my life. Never let anyone steal my black boy joy. She said being black is special. She said being black makes you cool.

"So tomorrow when that kid comes back, I want you to ignore him. Can you do that?"

"I'll try."

The next day, "Hey Adrian, your hair is so mmm ugly like you." I just kept walking, and I showed no emotion on my face. Eventually he ended up stopping. He didn't even talk to me.

But just think if I had never told my mother. It'd probably still be happening. I want this story to inspire you. Never let anyone steal your black boy joy. And also trust your mother— she's the best to talk to. And never let anyone bring you down.

Adrian L.
   Age 10

Surprise!

It was January 12, a normal day to others. But to me it was *the day*. The best day in history. My BIRTHDAY! I really wanted a phone. I was watching Young Sheldon.

Then suddenly, someone knocked on my door. I said *Who is ittttt?*

The mysterious person said, *It's Auntie Vi*ta. I opened the door and it was! She came in and gave me a gift, but she wouldn't let me open it until the rest of the family arrived. I thought it was a race car.

My mom came in after her. With the cake in her hand. *Eeee!* I was so excited and filled with Joy. Then my entire family arrived,and it was time. The old 9-year old self was gone. Bring in the new and improved 10 year old!

Alijah E.
    Age 10

Third Grade Friends

In 2018 to 2019, I was in third grade. I had multiple best friends such as Kijah, Khishawn, Quinn, Allen, and Clark. I also had the best/nicest Teacher.

One time, I was to play a game called "Silent Ball". This game meant you had to be quiet and throw a ball. One time we were playing for a Magic Jordan card! I came in second and got it, and she give this son a Magic Jordan card.

Then Covid hit very, very, very hard. My school shut down. Virtual learing was fun, but then the school year ended.

Me, mom, and dad went TGI Fridays. After we sat down, we started talked about switching schools. I was so sad, but at least my mom works there. But I was still nervous.

Alijah E.
Age 10

My Finger

One day in third grade I was trying to be the line leader. I put my finger by the door and somebody shut it. My finger was gray, and I almost passed out! I started yelling my teacher's name, and she looked mad that I was not raising my hand. Then she looked at my finger and told me to go to the nurse.

Walking out of the room with tears, I went to the nurse and she called my mom. But my mom works as a teacher, and she was subbing for a class, so she couldn't pick me up. My mom started crying over the phone. Then she called my uncle and grandpa to come and pick me up.

While I was waiting— as every nurse does— she told me to put some ice on it. It felt like my uncle came in the blink of an eye. He told me he was going as fast as he could to pick me up. This day was also Friday the 13th, the same day my uncle got out of jail. I went to my grandma's house with my grandpa. I talked to my other uncle on the phone, so happy and surprised that he got out of jail.

I went to my grandpa's room and rested my eyes after 10 minutes. My grandma and grandpa checked on me. There was white stuff on my finger, so I put the Band-Aid back on.

After a couple hours, my dad came to pick me up. I went to the hospital, and they signed me in. Then my mom came in crying. Then they told me that I had to get my nail taken off. Me and my mom were talking about how I should or shouldn't get this done. Then I agreed with my mom, but I was super scared.

They put a numbing shot in my finger, and I was super scared of the big needle. The first one hurt, but none of the others did. Then

I got the fingernail taken off and they put Band-Aids all around my hand. Then after we left I went to see my uncle.

Aubrie U.
   Age 11

BLACK and PROUD

So one day I was excited to learn the past and learn the changes over the years. So at this time, I was at a mostly all Black private school, and we learned a lot about the past.

So I was wondering why, mostly some white people, not all, were racist back then? So then I was like— *Well hold on!*— that's not fair, you know?

So then I looked at the timelines going to the present where we are now, and I learned people stood up for themselves. People for example like, Dr Martin Luther King Jr, Malcolm X, Rosa Parks, and Madam CJ Walker.

And now you're wondering,

Aubrie, you haven't told us why you're Black and Proud?

Well, I'll tell you I am Black and Proud.

I'm BLACK and PROUD.
   Some people are still racists, especially
   talking to
   You know, Karens.
   But I've learned that
   It doesn't matter what skin color you are.
   And that's why,
   I'm BLACK and PROUD!

Aubrie U.
  Age 11

The Day I Lost Someone

As days go by
  And time flies by
  Out there was someone special, but sadly
  she died
  I cried and
  I cried as how she had died
  And all the words I chose for a question was
  Why? Why? Why?
  I hoped she was with Jesus because I like to
  pray but all I could say was
  Hope you're alright
  As days go, my sadness faded
  But all I could do was Pray, Pray, Pray
  As I slept and slept
  And ate and ate
  As I got happier, I had one sentence to say as
  I sat by her grave
  The sentence I had to say was
  Hope you're okay

This poem is dedicated to my Auntie.

Austin U.
  Age 10

Good Days

I remember when I was sad, so sad. My dad...I did not see him for a long time until he came. He said, *Can I come with him?* And I said sure, so he took me to the mall to play games and get shoes. We got cinnamon pretzel—they're my favorite. I got white and green Kyries. We went to gamestop, and he got me some Xbox cards.

Then we went home and I hugged my mom.

Austin U.
    Age 10

Hardest Thing

So I was at school, and we went to lunch. We were about to go to recess. And I was playing with my buddy, but then I got a new buddy and then my old buddy was mad. Then I played with my old buddy, and my new buddy got mad. The hardest thing was that I couldn't be friends with both of them because they thought I had to choose. I felt depressed. Why do I have to choose?

Austin U.
    Age 10

The Needle

I remember when I was scared a long time ago. I was 5 years old, and I went downstairs at my grandma's house. I fell down the stairs and a needle got stuck in my ankle. I screamed my grandma's name so loud, *GRANDMA!*

My two cousins saw me fall down the stairs, so they told my grandma what happened. My grandma pulled the needle out of my ankle, wiped it off, and put it back in the stairs, so it could be stable. She gave me a white square bandage that I kept on for months. It didn't take long for me to heal and walk again. And that is how I got a needle in my ankle.

Bryson I.

Age 11

Mom's Macaroni

What's good to me? Definitely food! But the best food my mom makes is macaroni. And it's just so special and hot when it comes out the oven. It's so gooey and cheesy! it just makes my mouth water thinking about it. And she puts a bunch of cheddar cheese, and she makes it so creamy. When you bite into it… well, that's when the fun starts! When my mom makes the macaroni, you can hear her stir the pot and sing.

Bryson I.

Age 11

I Did it!

By the name you know the main character is a cop that made a deal with the devil. Then the game starts with the first boss battle, a camp, onion, and a cow. This level was so hard that I stopped for the week. Then in the final battle with the devil, I had a death encounter, and it said 70. He was just too strong! I couldn't take it, but I didn't give up so I tried and tried and tried and I did it!

Bryson W.

Age 10

Covid Poem

Snoozing all day was kinda fun
but now I'm happy to be in the sun.
The vaccine changed everything up,
had me feeling like, *What up?*

The toilet paper wars were kinda dumb,

but it had me feeling kinda glum.
Scared for my grandparents to get sick.
They had to pick if they wanted to
go to the doctors or stay sick.

Bryson W.
   Age 10

                    Memories

Since you asked I tell you why I'm tired...

Last night was a ball; we up till dawn.
   Thinking about old memories
   had a toll on me.
   Remembering the time my step sister threw
   up watermelon,
   had the whole house smellin'.
   The time I trapped my mom in the closet,
   my dad told me to lock it.
   Fourth of July, I really had fun
   but the fireworks made me run.
   All these memories mean so much to me,
   my family tree is really all that.
   Memories, memories, memories,
   they're the things that define us.
   Sometimes you have to find
   them deep in your mind.
   People say that if you don't
   remember memories, that they
   didn't matter to you.
   But that's just a straight up lie.
   Just because you don't remember
   your memories doesn't mean
   you don't care about them.
   Some memories are not that important,

but others are.
Like I said before,
my sister threw up watermelon.
That's a funny memory.
Funny memories stay with you,
but good ones don't.
It's a weird concept.
Your favorite memories disappear within
days,
but bad memories stay with you.
It's like a guilt trip all through your life.
Once that guilt ends,
you feel relieved.
Like you did something and had a purpose
in your life.
Once you die, your memories carry on
through heaven
and forever on.

Caden D.
    Age 12

Happiness

Since you asked I will tell you why I am happy. I am happy because I am at camp. I also am happy when I am playing sports. I am also happy when I play video games. I also am happy when I get money. I also am happy when I am at my grandmother's house. I am happy when I am with my cousins and family. I also am when I am with my friends.

Caden D.
   Age 12

ISTEP

The hardest thing I did was ISTEP. It is the yearly test that we take at the end of the year to see what we learned. Nobody likes it at the end of the year because we want to have fun instead of taking a test. But we have to do it anyway. And if we fail? You can get held back or have to take summer school. During the test, it was boring and annoying. But during the process I was happy when I was done. Once everyone is done, we can go do what we want.

Caden D.
   Age 12

My Surprise

A time when I was surprised was when I got a PS5. It was on a Tuesday after my basketball game. I went in the house, then into the kitchen where I got food then went into the basement. And there it was, sitting in the box. I was so excited that I was jumping and running in the house. I opened it and plugged all the cords in; it took me an hour to do it, but I figured it out. I stayed up on it till 11 or 12 at night. So I was just playing free games cause I didn't have any yet. But it is cool, and I love to play with my friends. And the graphics are better. The games are fun and I always play with my friend.

Caleb M.
   Age 13

I Am Bored

Since you asked, I am bored. Bored because of COVID-19 and being quarantined. Bored because of COVID, people aren't able to create movies and video games like they used to.

Caleb M.
   Age 13

My Dog

A time when I lost something very special to me was my dog Gracie. I am from Mississippi, and in Mississippi it's more country than city so it was hard to take care of a pet. We had Gracie for 10 years, and she was loved throughout the whole family. My aunt gave her to us.

She was missing for a few days so we decided to go into the woods to look for her. We found her but she was acting weird. She was sitting down. And when we called her, she would not come. So we took her to the house and found out she got bit by a snake. My mom nursed on her. She was okay for a few days, but died after two days.

Middle School

Something that was hard for me was going to Middle school. It was hard because of the classes. Math was the hardest. Things were different from Elementary and it took me a while to get used to the program but eventually I did.

Core Counselor Erica

What Happened in 2020

What I think about COVID 19? A hurtful and very damaging disease that cause so many symptoms, our nation became severely ill. Within weeks so many Fathers, Mothers, Aunties, Uncles, Brothers, Sisters died. My Uncle Jimmy Woods only lived for a week, and I thought to myself, *Why did he have to die?*

Because of this illness. He never did even come outside, but one of his nurses gave him the COVID. I am very mad about our nation's decision, because I truly think this could have been prevented.

I have heard some damaging news. What I do think when I hear doctors and nurses speak about this pandemic? I truly believe I should follow my heart. I am alive and alert about my surroundings. I haven't decided on my shot and I don't want to be judged based on a shot that wasn't FDA approved.

Core Counselor Erica

Dear Families and Me,

This pandemic had me talking to myself, and I wasn't going to give up. I have decided to process on with this challenge. So many thoughts have gone on in my head so this is what I have came up with:

1. Do better than the day before.
2. Go back to school.
3. Make my life better with the Lord.
4. Work on financials.
5. Buy a HOUSE.
6. Being single never hurt anyone.
7. I am not perfect, but I will give my very best.
8. I have seen so many hurtful things in my life.
9. My life is not finished.

I Questioned Everything During Covid

I questioned everything I did during Covid such as getting up before 7 am, making sure all my chores were done, my bath, cooking to find out that I could do everything before I go out the door.

So about three weeks into the pandemic, I just had so many questions. I called my mother, and I told her that sitting in this house with no furniture, just my blown up bed and it was driving me crazy.

See, what I didn't tell you was that I caught my kitchen on fire on August 23, 2019. Not having nothing in my home and nothing to keep me active drove me crazy.

Before I called my mama, I called the Wayne Township Clinic, and they didn't answer the call so I thought that was a sign from God to call my mama.

Of course my mama kicked into full gear.

There is nothing wrong with you! Until I tell you you're crazy, you think of nothing! If you want to talk, just talk.

What really came to my mind was no self time with me.

So some things have changed now for me. The pandemic changed me.

Core Counselor Mya

Mya,

Be as sweet as the first day you met you.
That first recollected memory that you have.
The first time that you realized that you are real. Things will happen in your life,
But don't blame yourself for the things that don't go right.
It's not your fault people think you're hard to love,
They cracked open your chest to get to your heart,

Forgive me I get a little emotional about this part,
I know that Dog walked all over that organ.
Don't get hard though.
The world is your oyster,
You are a pearl.
Don't harden your heart,
Just because this is a cold cruel world,
That choked you and flipped you over—
YOU
Have to pick up your bootstraps and get protected,
So you send a threat here,
And want to fight there,
And you pierced your nose,
And you cut your hair,
JUST so you can feel something,
But you can't.
But you still can't feel anything.
You're numb,
You're not dumb,
You're sad,
And your body's natural response is to react,
However you can.
So hold your head up!
You're doing the best that you can!

Core Counselor Mya

Scared

Okay, so when I was 14, I was on a rollercoaster at the state fair. It was *the* rollercoaster, the one that goes around in a circle. At the beginning, the guy was playing with the buttons, so off tops, I should have known that this old "do you wanna play carnival games?" lookin man was about to be on straight foolishness.

Okay, so anyway, the rollercoaster finally starts, then after it goes for a few minutes, I thought that he was about to stop it, so I took off my seatbelt, and the rollercoaster went around again.

So, a part of me was scared, but the other part of me loved the thrill.

Dalaysia G.
    Age 13

The Razor

I remember the time when I was in the shower. I had just hopped out the shower and decided to discover the bathroom. I opened one of the cabinets, and I found a razor. When I found the razor, I decided to shave my leg to see what it felt like.

So, I started to shave my leg. It was going well then *BOOM!* A patch of skin came off my leg! Blood dripped down my leg. I started feeling light-headed. I started to get scared because I knew my mom was going to punish me for using a razor.

I thought of a master plan. I was gonna tell her that I scraped myself on the faucet. I started feeling even more light-headed. Long story short, I got about 60 stitches because the wound was that big.

Darion S.
    Age 11

When My Grandpa Died

My grandpa died April 2nd 2021. He was 95, turning 96 on June 6. He was born in 1925. He died of a heart stroke. He went to the doctor, and his heart was pumping 170/0. Your heart has to pump at least 560/0.

Now I'm gonna tell you the relationship I had with him. We really were not that close, but I went to the grocery store with him and my grandma. And when he was on Earth, I always use to mess with him. And he could still run fast at 95 years old. And I went to the funeral, and it was sad seeing him in a casket.

Darion S.
    Age 11

A Time I Got Really Scared

So my cousin plays football. He was 13 when this happened. He is 15 turning 16 in October. So football runs in my family. So he was in his championship game. His team name was the Brownsburg Bulldogs, and the team he was facing was the Louisiana Lobsters.

And one of his friends on the other team hit him in his head, and his helmet fell off and he fell to the ground really hard so we rushed to the hospital. His heart was beating really slowly, and it was hard for him to breathe.

So they took us out of the room. And one of the doctors came out and told us in a few hours, your family member will be dead. So everybody started crying. Then we left. And then a few days later the same doctor said he had good news. It turned out that he was just in a coma for 3 days.

Dee A.S.
    Age 13

My Sister Aashaya

On November 23, 2019 my sister Aashaya was driving in the car, and A bullet hit her and she died. She has 3 kids, Lamiya, TJ, and Taylor. Me and my sister were really close even though she was 27 years old.

My favorite memory with my sister is when I went to her house, she cooked us breakfast and we all made a musical dance video. I always enjoyed going to get our nails done together with my niece Lamiya. I will always cherish the memories that we had.

The colors we were wearing to the funeral were black and red. The church had white walls and stained colored windows with a purple cross. The seats were wooden and purple.

Now every 23rd of each month, we have a black, red, and white balloon release And visit her grave. And today on the 23rd, I'm not able to be there.

Dee A.S.
   Age 13

Word Party

Word party entered my life from my 2-year old niece, Jhream. I used to babysit her every Friday and that's all she likes—Word Party. Word Party is a show with animals in it like pandas and elephants.

The animals talk to the kids and be like: *It's time for lunch.* and *It's time for recess.* They also sing. When somebody's sad, they sing to cheer them up. They sing about recess, food, all of that.

I wasn't annoyed by it; it was interesting to me. I watched it with her, and I started getting into it because it was interesting. It played all the time, 24/7, and my niece started to sound like the animals.

I really like when the animals try to cheer people up. My favorite animals are the cheetah, panda, and elephant, but I like all of them. They're pretty cool. I like all of the songs on Word Party and Cocomelon.

Maybe I'm around kids too much.

Enyae G.
Age 13

Since You Asked...

Since you asked, I'll tell you why I'm happy. My favorite show came back on so that's good. I'm also happy because I got new shoes and clothes. I'm also happy because I'm going to King's Island this summer. I went 2 years ago. I'm happy because I am going swimming this weekend or maybe this Friday. Since you asked, I'll tell you why I'm happy. I got new head scarfs/turbans to wear like one I got on now. Since you asked, I'll tell you why I'm mad. I broke my XBox, and I can't play games anymore. I am mad my Doritos are gone.

Since you asked, I tell you why I'm loved. I am loved because my mom cares for me and makes me feel confident. I am loved by my brother because I am accompanied, and he makes sure I am protected. I feel loved by my grandma because when we come over, we get nice food and go to places like the pool. Since you asked, I feel loved by my whole family because they care for me and make sure I feel loved and accompanied.

Enyae G.
Age 13

My Hair

My hair is naturally curly. When I go swimming, my hair shrinks. I get my hair done every day, and it always hurts. My hair hurts because the brushes pull my hair, and it feels like my hair is being pulled out.

I love how long my hair is when it's being straightened out, and it looks healthy. My hair shrinks when it's wet, and when it's dry, it goes back to its regular length.

I want my hair to grow to my back when I get older. I usually make sure I do my hair every day, so it grows. I have hair wash days, but the water gets inside my hairs and ears and I get so annoyed. I get my ends cut every other month, sometimes at least 1 time a month —it helps kill dead ends so your hair can grow. My hair is sometimes braided, twisted and down. I love my hair and most things about it, but some days not so much. My hair is sandy brown, and in the sun it's light-ish brown. I love my sandy brown curly hair :)

Faith A.
  Age 12

Why I Love Being Black

I love being Black because of how my hair is, and how I can style it in different ways. Another reason I love being Black is because of June 19th or Juneteenth. Juneteenth is very Important to the Black community. And how there are different shades of Black people like Brown skin, Dark skin, and Light skin.

Faith A.
  Age 12

The Struggle with my Hair

My hair struggle is real, especially when I don't have braids in my hair. When you have thick hair like me, it's very hard to do even when your hair is flat ironed because you have to wrap it. Because if you don't, your hair will sweat back and go back to it's natural stages. The end.

Faith A.
  Age 12

Who Was Good to Me

There was a time in 6th grade that I had a favorite teacher. She was my English teacher, and how she was good to me was because everytime I needed help, she would help me. Then there was a club named P.E.A.R.L.S., and I wasn't going to sign up for it but my teacher signed me up. I don't know how, but she did. And the club was actually fun! We went Ice skating, and to the Grand Lux Cafe. When I got in 7th grade, I sent her an email thanking her for all the help.

The end.

Graham A.
  Age 11

Things I Do

1. I watch Anime HXH, Demon Slayer, and more
2. I play football my fave position is WR
3. I play video games and anime games
4. I eat Ramon— chicken flavor
5. I have fun spending time with family and friends

Graham A.
  Age 11

How I Fell Down the Stairs

I was walking upstairs, and I had a laptop in my hand. And when I was walking down the stairs, I fell and I hurt my leg. I had a rug burn, but it healed after two days. The laptop just closed and wasn't broken.

My mom and my sister heard me fall, but we all laughed. We laugh every time someone falls down the stairs and isn't hurt bad. No one has gotten really hurt after falling down the stairs.

Isaiah M.
   Age 10

Why I'm Angry

Since you asked Ima tell you why I'm angry. well to start off, I was supposed to go to school at 7:30. I wake up 10:30, and when I got to school, I had to sit in detention until 12:30 and could not have my reccess.

And when it was time to go, I had to stay back for 3 hours since I was 3 hours late. Then my mom found out that I was late, and she was mad because she has to leave her job to pick me up. Then she was mad at me and grounded me, so now I can't play late at night at all because I was three hours late. That's why I don't stay up late anymore. That was the worst last day of school, and this happened when I was on the last day of school.

Isaiah M.
   Age 10

Living With My Uncle and Auntie

I went to go live with my auntie and uncle because my mom and dad had to go to different states, and I decided to go live with my uncle and auntie. I felt okay about my mom and dad leaving because I was going to go live with my aunt and uncle.

I would call my parents like every day when I was at my uncles and my auntie house. I love to play with my cousins. We would play board games, PS4 games, and we would go outside and just run around in the yard.

When my parents got back, I did not want to go so I stayed for the rest of the summer. Then when I had to go, I gave my auntie and uncle a Big Hug. And when we was on our way to my mamma and dad's house, and I told my mom and dad so many stories. They loved my stories, and when we got home I was so happy to be back home.

James G.
Age 10

2020 Pandemic

In 2020, there was, of course, Covid-19 and it happened in February of 2020. And I remember watching TV, and I heard of something called Covid-19 and I thought nothing of it. But then a few months later, we had to wear masks and do to this day. I remember March 17th, we had to go to school that day but it got cancelled, and I never went to school again.

And then basketball stopped because of the spread of Covid-19, and I haven't played since. And then in April, I lost most of my friends to Covid-19. But in September 2020, I was depressed for a few months but I powered through it. But in 2021, I hope everything goes back to normal. Thank you for reading this.

Sincerely, James

P.S: I love the Writers Center.

Editor's Note: We love you too, James!

James G.
  Age 10

Racist Teacher

In 4th grade, our teacher got sick and we had a substitute teacher. And the first few days were good, but then the last day on Friday, she blamed my classmate, Landon, because we had asked for a color because we were doing a project.

And then it started... one week later. it happened again with my friends Daniel, Keirien, Jadam, and me. We all got in trouble with the sub. And got sent to the principal and one month later, we reported her to the principal.

We found out that she is racist and didn't like black people or any other people of color. And when our teacher came back, we told her what happened, and she told us are we okay. But then 2 years later, we are fighting to get her out of are school system.

But in Oct. 27, 2020, she said she was sorry and apologized to everyone that was in my class. and at first I'm like, *Should I accept her apology?* But then I did because I was like *Keep your family close, but keep your enemies closer.*

James G.
  Age 10

My Grandma

So I'll tell you why I'm sad. In May of 2015, my grandma passed away when I was 5 years old. She died at 93 years old, and she would always say, *100 days of school.* Because when she used to say this to my mom when she was little, she'd say *You have 100 days of school.*

And then she said to herself, *100 days of school,* hoping she'd live to be 100 years old. And then we went to her funeral. And at first, I was shocked when I heard the news. And after that, they did the service, and I cried so hard that day I was so sad. And the song that they played at the funeral was

"See You Again" by Wiz Khalifa. And every time they play it I cry.

P.S. Love you, Grandma Gigi.

Jathen T.
    Age 12

$5 Dollar Bill

The time I lost something that meant a lot to me, something that made me feel good about myself. It made me feel like I was rich!

I lost my 5 dollars. I was heartbroken. I was so sad. I was only 8 when it happened. I was too young to lose something that great.

I was mad too, but then one day, I looked in the couch and found my 5 dollars and then I was happy again.

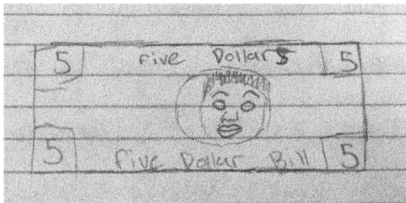

Jathen T.
Age 12

Scared

My story is gonna be about how I got scared. It was a normal Saturday, and I was in the car with my friend and his brother and his dad on our way to a football game. When we got there, my friend and his brother —we were looking for somewhere to sit down. When we sat down, we watched the game for a bit then got up to get some food from the concession stands.

When we got to the concession stands, we got the food then went back to sit down. When we was finished with our food, me and my friend we went to the sidelines to play some football with some other people— I really didn't know who they were but it was okay.

So on one play, I was running and I bent and broke my toe. When I broke my toe, I really didn't know it was broke— but it did hurt. After the game, my friends dad took me to my grandma's house. I Facetimed my mom to tell her about my hurting toe; she said it might be broke and not to walk on it. She said she will pick me up in the morning and take me to the doctor, but when she picked me up she did not take me to the doctor. Instead we went to my uncle's house for a pool party. Since we did not go to the doctor I didn't know what was wrong with my toe. I made it worse that day.

When it hit nighttime, we finally went to the ER. When we got to the room, the doctor took X-Rays to tell if it was broke. The doctor came back with answers and it broke— I was mad. The doctor said not to walk on it and gave me crutches. It scared me really bad. The weekend started good, then ended not so good.

Jay B.
    Age 10

Great-Grandparents

The hardest thing in my life was when my great grandparents died. One died from old age, and the other one died from being sick. And at the funeral, I cried at the end because I could not see her. And we had a feast after, and it probably weighed more than me.

Jay B.
    Age 10

Being Black

I love being Black because:

- Hair
- I am different because I have six dimples
- All soul food
- Clothes
- Basketball, track, football, soccer

Jay B.
    Age 10

The Day Archie Died

This is about the time when my cousin's dog died. His name is Archie. He was a mixed breed. He was a good dog because he listened to us. When I said, *Don't go into the kitchen*. He did. He played a lot.

Archie died of old age. I think he was 10 or 11 years old. When I found out that he died, I cried.

Jeffrey A.
    Age: 12

Since You Asked

Since you asked, I'll tell you why I'm angry. I'm angry when people ask me how my mom passed away because it's kinda disrespectful, and I don't feel like talking about it.

Since you asked, I'll tell you why I'm angry. When I'm mad at people, I just feel, I don't know it just feels bad.

Since you asked, I'll tell you why I'm angry. When my friends are not online, and I have to play with people I don't know. And when my game has to update, because I have to wait a long time to play it again.

Jeffrey A.
    Age 12

My Long Black Hair

I'm gonna tell you about my good, long, black hair. When I go out with my hair, I like to pull it and twist it a lot, because it's my black hair. I hate it when my dad cuts my hair down, because I want my hair to grow more. When he cuts it down, some people like it.

But I love when he lets me grow it out, and let it be so it can be long and great. I love after I take a shower and my hair is long and curly. I love when I get compliments about my good, long, black hair.

I love my black hair.

Joi R.
    Age 11

How Joi Celebrates Her Black Girl Joy

I celebrate by having a great imagination. I like to draw. I have a sketchbook where I have all my drawings.

Sometimes, I talk to myself because I have problems talking to people, and I have trust issues. I used to have Tourette's syndrome. People used to tease me for being like that. Like for example, I used to tick every time I talked.

But now people just bully me, because I'm fat or because I'm black.

But I know I'm Black, and I'm proud. Even after losing my mom and dad, I'm okay.

Joi R.
    Age 11

My Mother

My mother was the best thing that ever happened to me. That was until she died. Her death was February 3, 2021. They say that there are five steps of depression and grief: denial, anger, bargaining, depression, and acceptance.

Well, all of these are me. Denial was the first one, I didn't, couldn't believe my family when they told me about her death.

Anger was the second one, I started to lash out on everyone I know.

Bargaining was the third, I pushed away my sadness and started to say *What if?* scenarios.

Depression was the fourth, I started to talk to myself and be alone all the time.

And finally, acceptance, I don't know what to say about this one. Let's just say I'm not there yet.

I haven't accepted her death.

Jordan T.
    Age 10

I Always Do

I always see my brothers.
    I always shower.
    I always go home.
    I always sleep.
    I always wake up.
    I always see my dog everyday. Her name is
Dory, and she is a Black lab.
    I always put clothes on.
    I always see my mom.
    I always see me.
    I always see my refrigerator.
    I always see my deep freezer.
    I always see my bathroom.

Jordan T.
    Age 10

The Not-So-Hot Tub

When I was watching a movie called *Creed*, he fell in the pool and I said I wanted to go to the pool. My mother said we might go to the hotel, and we did. And when we got there I was saying it was my fault because I wanted to go to the pool. My mother agreed. And I said, *I told you, it's my fault we was here.*

My brother said, *All right, all right!*

So we started swimming, hot tubbing, and in two hours and a half later, we had to get out of the pool. I got on my Nintendo Switch playing Fortnite and I got bored of my friends, so I went to sleep. And I wake up and I got ready to go to the pool, and I realized the hot tub was closed! We were playing football in the water, and one of my brothers threw it in the hot tub that was closed. We went and got it and saw that the water wasn't hot.

Juliana M.
    Age 10

Since You Asked, I'll Tell You Why I'm Happy

Since you asked, I'll tell you why I'm happy. I'm happy because I got 2 baby ducks. They were yellow and soft. There so cute! The day I got the ducks, I won a picture in a game of Bingo at my school.

Another reason why I'm happy? Because my mom cooked fish— which is my favorite food. A third reason why I'm happy is because days and days later, I got two more baby ducks! And after a few days later, I got a new dog

Here is how I got my new dog. One day when I was at home and the sun was out and I was watching TV in my room. It started to get dark. I went out of my room to get something to drink and when I opened the door and was walking by, I saw my mom holding a cute little dog in her hands. *I gasped!* The puppy was so cute! After that, my mom told me how she got the puppy. She said that one of her co-workers gave it to her for free, and then I said, *That was a good deal.* We ended up naming her Bella. She is a weiner dog.

Juliana M.
    Age 10

Something That Makes Me Happy About Being Black.

Something that makes me happy about being Black is my hair. My hair can be curly. It can be fluffy. It can be silky. It can be smooth.

Another thing that makes me happy about being Black is that I can't get a sunburn. Another thing? I come from a race where there were important people that changed the world for the sake of Black lives around the world.

Kevin P.
    Age 10

Losing a Best Friend

The day I lost my best friend, it was hard time. It was a hard for me. It was a year ago that we were playing and I told my mom told me I was mad because we had to move in a month. My mom and dad, they start fighting. Two weeks later I hear fighting again, then we had to move. That day got me depressed. I needed therapy, but I talked to my big Sis who has helped me to this day, but I still feel the pain of losing my best friend and moving.

Kevin P.
    Age 10

The Boogie-Man

It was on April Fools, unlike any other day. On that day, a prank happened. It made me pee my pants! The Boogie-man came out and he was wearing a mask.

Leonard C.
Age 13

My Dad

My Dad is good to me because he has a good personality. He has a good mindset every day. We have a strong relationship, but it could be stronger. He gets me things I want and need. He is overall a good person. In fact, it has gotten stronger over the years.

Leonard C.
Age 13

Surprise

One day I was getting dropped off at my house and was watching TV with my cousins and my other cousin. And then, we went to the store. Then my big cousin pulled up. When he pulled up. He had his dirtbike! And we started riding the dirt bike. And then he left it with me for a couple hours, and he came back and took it home.

Makayla A.
Age 11

My Experience Through The...Pandemic!

It all started when my mom picked me up from school. When I got in the car, she was on the phone and she said to the person on the phone I am going to tell her now. And when she got off the phone, she told me that Iwas out of school due to Covid, and at first I thought that was a good thing.

But it was not. It was WRONG, very wrong. The first few days were good, but then those days turned into weeks and those weeks turned into months and those months turned into boredom. and after that, they came up with e-learning and I was kinda sad because I missed my friends and I still do.

Makayla A.
    Age 11

Ending A Friendship

The hardest thing I have ever done... was to end the best friendship of my life. It all started when I walked into class, and I saw my best friend and she looked really sad like she was about to cry. So I went up to her and asked her what was wrong. When I asked her what was wrong, she then said that she was moving and at first I did not think it was that bad but then she told me that she was moving to Florida!

And at that moment that's when my whole world ended. When I got home that day, all I did was cry, cry, and cry. The next day at school, I brought her a moving away basket. I put a card with some stickers — since she loved stickers— some food shaped erasers and a friendship bracelet.

The day came when I came to school, she was nowhere to be found and the same thing happened the next day and the next day. That's when I found out she already moved... but over the past 2 years, we have been writing each other. And then one day, she stopped writing to me and then I stopped writing to her but me and her both know we would give anything to see each other again.

Malik M.
    Age 13

Constructive Criticism

Dealing with a stranger's constructive criticism is definitely easier than dealing with constructive criticism from your friends and family. That might just be my opinion, but I feel like criticism from close friends just hits different. Because if a stranger says something about me, trying to be nice but helpful it doesn't really affect me because they don't know me personally. But if my best friend said the same thing to me? Then I would feel a little hurt because they would know everything about me. And if they know everything about me, and they feel this way then what do the people that don't know me feel like.

Malik
   Age 13

Best Friend

Just another random day in math class. I was bored and sitting on the only other bouncy ball in the classroom. I was in third grade, and it was like the second week of school and we were about to start our first problem of the day. And then Ethan walked in looking like he didn't wanna be there, and it was school so, he didn't. When Ethan walked in, the teacher said that we were doing partner work, and I instantly wanted to be his partner because he was the new kid and he was mysterious.

When we picked partners, me and Ethan were not, no, we were never ever partners, and it made me mad because we had the same partners all year. And I had been stuck with Christopher, ugh. I really couldn't stand him at all because we were always arguing, because he couldn't do anything right. And it irritated me so much, because the teacher wouldn't change our partners. Me and Ethan were friends, but we got really close in the fourth grade.

Matthew A.
Age 10

YBA

1. Yba or Your Bizarre Adventure has too short of a storyline.

1. When someone's time stops, it freezes people and it has the biggest range.

1. Golden experience requiem can make time stop go away.

1. Tusk Act 4 takes way too long to get to.
2. First, you need you spin.
3. Second, you need to lift the arm of the pelvis.
4. Third, you need to talk to Jesus, and
5. Finally, you need a pelvis to get Tusk Act 4.

1. Yba has way too many codes, but only prestige III can use them.

1. The start of a long, long long grind for White Snake. Getting White Snake is not a walk in the park to get. It's a 1% chance— One Percent! Do you know how rare that is?! But after countless hours on edge, the arrow that would change my life. One arrow stab later… White Snake appears. The hunt that lasted three whole days has came to end.

Matthew A.
    Age 10

People Who Been Good To Me

1. My mom because she always tries to help me.
2. My cousins are good to me, because we all agree on things and we play a bunch of games.
3. My dad is good to me. He calls me every once in a while, and I'm happy to see him through Facetime.
4. My grandparents are good to me because they get me cool toys, and they are always happy.

Mianna S.
    Age 13

Black Girl Joy

I'm Black and I'm proud.
My name is Mianna, and I see
a lot of racism go on in
the world and I also see a lot
of riots going on as well.
And I actually participated in one
of the protesting, and I'm glad I did.
I love my hair type, I love
my skin color, and I went to
the protest downtown, and I had
a sign that said
Black Lives Matter.

Mianna S.
Age 13

Black Hair Life

A time when my Black life didn't matter was when I went to Kindergarten at my school. There was mostly white kids at my school, and most of my teachers were white. My friends used to always ask me about my hair, and why it was so short and curly and always in braids. And I didn't know what to say but *My mom likes it that way.*

I always wanted to wear my down and straight like my friends. So I told my mom I wanted to wear it down one day, so she braided it overnight, and took it down in the morning and my hair was staying down and I loved it!

So I went to school, and I showed my friends my hair and they liked it. So I started wearing my hair like that all the time. But after a while, it got tiring so I went back to my braids and puff balls and had to realize my hair isn't like everybody's, so I just had to deal with it.

Mikayle H.
Age 13

Being Black I

Sometimes I just question my own race because most people will come up to you and say, *Oh, your hair is ugly or your hair is short..* And sometime, it will be the people you thought were your friends. And half of the time, they do not know the struggle of coarse hair. Some girls' hair is curly, some straight, some short, some long, but also they have to deal with maintaining the hair they have.

Being Black II

Being Black is hard.

Being Black comes with a card.
Being Black is a success.
Being Black can cause stress.
When you're Black,
You get judged.
But being Black--
is JOY.
That's why you
Have to be Proud.
Because we have
To fight for each other,
Because we are all
Sisters and Brothers.

Being Black III

Being black should not be hard, but in the world we are in today? It is very difficult. Mainly dealing with racism and all the hatred towards each other. We can't really go anywhere without white people looking at you different because of the color on your skin. But not everyone will judge you based off your skin color.

Naomi M.
    Age 11

Skyzone

We got to Skyzone and did the usual registration and signing in stuff. I went to the trampoline first, as usual. I bounced around and bumped into someone. I got elbowed in the chest. Then I went over to the rope ladder where you have to press the buzzer twice to fall down. My feet slipped so I was hanging the whole time, but I hit the buzzer. Can't take me down! The rock climbing is in the corner of the building. I went on the rock climbing wall. My hands started hurting, but I was still climbing. I thought to myself *Why did I do this? Why did I climb up here?"* I had to jump down because there was no other way to get down. So I had to jump.

Naomi M.
Age 11

My Hair

I like when my mom straightens my hair. It's fun. But when I'm in the pool, I want it to be curly. It will turn curly anyway, but I don't mind it. It's nice to have my hair out once in a while. So yeah, I like my hair. You got a problem with that?

Saniia F.
Age 10

Karens

Karens discriminate.

Karens do stuff for clout, like they'll go inside a restaurant or a store without a mask just to argue with people. Karens are clout-chasers. They like to argue with people for no reason. They can't mind they own business.

They are a disgrace to me.

They always wanna say, *I'm gonna record you guys.*

So, what had happened was, I was taking out the trash and she was like, *Why are you throwing all that trash on the ground?*

And then she started recording me.

I was confused because I didn't even do nothing, and my mom was like, *Are you recording my daughter?*

She was like *Yes, I am!*

My mom said, *In Indiana, it is illegal to record someone's child without their permission. It is a law.*

I was mad.

Saniia F.
    Age 10

Racism

Travon Martin was 16 or 17 yrs old when he was shot by a racist man over a bag of Skittles. I thought that was messed up because the man thought Travon stole them.

Stop Racism.
    BLM
    We need to stop Racism.
    BLM 4 Life.
    Please stop Racism.

Sevan E.
    Age: 13

Black Girl Joy

My Black girl joy always shines through my beautiful black skin when I am with my people. My people bring out my Black Girl Joy. My people who are loved. My people who are kind. My people who are proud. My people who blow my mind. They bring out the best in me. Example when I get to the right level of hype at a cookout. I will have everyone on the floor getting their groove on. Sometimes my people can bring out the Black Girl Joy that gives me the strength to sass to tell someone off. With that being said, Black Girl Joy isn't always Joy. It can be

Black Girl Joy, Anger, or Strength. But through it all I embrace it.

Sevan E.
    Age 13

The Things I Do

The things I do are simple. Wake up to whining children at 6 in the morning. Then I get dressed and look in my mirror, and I do a little dance to hype myself up. As my mother calls for her children to get in the car like a major calling their newest soldier to training. The drive to camp is long and drawn out because of all of the excessive and unnecessary questions that are asked by the little "soldiers."

I doze off in the car, but the next thing you know we're at camp. Camp consists of a lot of things and are different everyday. Camp ends. But no time to rest, It's time for basketball and the stress of my teammates. We sweat, get yelled at, but it is all good fun. My mom picks me up, and I take a good shower, head on to sleep and then the day is done.

Sevan E.
    Age 13

The Hospital

Big, Bright, White Lights. My mother with her 'strong' face in the hospital chair to my left, a heart monitor to my right, my nanny laying still in her possible death bed is right in front of me. A big brown door with a brass handle is towering over my back. The floor is smooth like a marble countertop in a kitchen. The continuous beeping of the heart monitor is breaking the horrible silence of the grim hospital, the smell of hand sanitizer, and rubble gloves fill my nostrils up. The rough bumpy feel of the hospital blanket irritates my hands but I touch it anyways so long as I am comforting my nanny. The taste of chocolate hospital ice cream is still on the tip of my tongue, as I sit in the grim hospital.

Sonnie T.
   Age 13

To My Future Son

To my future son,

Boy, you got it good. As a 13 year old, I've witnessed over 600,000 people die from a virus, and no not the one in your computer. This virus is called Coronavirus, or how I like to say it Covid-19.

As you can see, it is pretty dangerous and one of the ways they said will prevent it is "wearing a cloth over your face." Which I don't think is very effective, because you have to wear a huge mask to paint.

That isn't the only hard thing. I am the oldest brother out of 3— I have an older sister, and she is an influence on me with the way she is doing big things at a young age. My brothers are trippin' me out man. Hopefully we can get more into detail, but just know it's hard fathering 3 half grown men.

School is normal for me, I'm currently going to 8th grade. And camp? I can't wait to send you to camp, and you tell me how it went.

One more thing I'd like to think that you should know? I'm a mama's boy— I love my mother very much. I have so much respect for my mom.

I can't wait to meet you.
   Sonnie

Sonnie T.
    Age 13

Don't Make Me Feel Like My Black Life Doesn't Matter

This story begins when my family went out to eat. We were getting ready to leave, and this white lady wanted to get past my brother, but she didn't say *Excuse me*. It made us pretty upset because that day? That day was the day after Juneteenth, so it made us feel like she thought that we owed her something.

On top of that, I held open the door so we could leave, and another white lady didn't say *Thank you*, and she looked at me like I *needed* to hold the door open for her. The fact that my ancestors have been through all of that for hundreds of years, people who have been stolen from their home, tricked on a ship, and enslaved for hundreds of years. It's so rude how some white people treat us like dirt. Well that's a time when someone made me feel like my black life didn't matter.

Sonnie T.
    Age 13

Sad

This is the time I lost someone that was important to me. On December 5, 2017, Cancer came back to take my granddad's life. When I got the news, my mom was picking up me and my brothers from an after-school program. When she told me, the only thing I could do was cover my mouth and cry. Even though he had Alzheimer's, I felt like everytime I would go to my grandma's house, he made the house more full.

I loved talking to him. Me and my cousins would feel his soft, smooth, warm, bald head. I remember when I was at his viewing, I felt his head one more time, and I jerked back when I felt his head was hard as a rock and cold. I miss my Paw Paw. He always smiled, and always cussed— which made me laugh. It's not the same going over my grandma's house and not seeing him. I miss him so much. I wish I could hear him cuss one more time. I wish I could feel his soft, smooth, warm, bald head one more time.

Sonnie T.
   Age 13

Scared

A time when I was scared was when my dad was in the hospital. A couple years ago my dad got an infection in his knee. The day he got it, he brought me and my brothers to work with him. He is an Air Conditioning tech guy that usually works inside, but on that day we were outside. He didn't have a knee pad. So he used a form of plastic, but over that time of working, he rubbed his knee on the plastic so much, his skin broke.

After a while he got tired of using it so he moved it, and his knee got cut in the dirt. So for everyone that told me to rub dirt on my cut? You're evil! So when he found out he had the infection, he went to the hospital to have surgery. My mom, brother, and sister went to go visit him after the surgery. It scared me when I saw him in the hospital bed. I couldn't even hug him. And that's the time something scared me.

Tazae H.
   Age 10

Pollution

Since you asked I will tell why I am angry. I am angry because of pollution. It hurts the earth. It hurts animals. It hurts insects. It hurts the air.

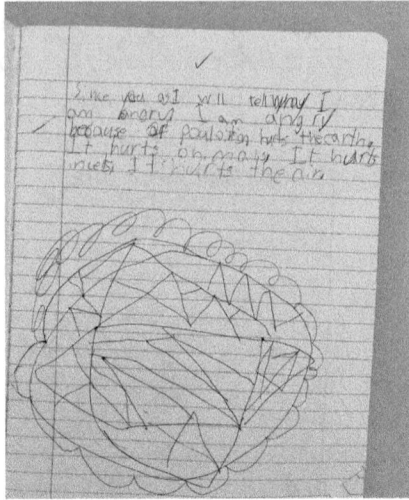

Tazae H.
    Age 10

A Day on MKXL

I play MKXL in my bedroom. I play by myself. Scorpion is the first thing I see. I press "X" to go into the game. I go to ranked matches. I choose my character. I like to choose Tony Cage, Spawn, or Baget Avatar. MKXL is so hard because everybody is good. One time I almost beat the person in 1st place. His health was blinking red, but then he comboed me!

Terreona J.
    Age 11

Don't Touch My Hair

When I was younger, my mom asked me if I wanted to just start getting my hair done in braids. I said *Yes*, because I've seen others with braids, and I thought it was pretty. Before then only my mom did my hair. Every day and no one said anything about it.

But when people first saw me in braids, they treated me differently. They would say, *Is that your real hair?It was so pretty*. They even started playing with it. They would braid it, twist it, and all different hairstyles.

Now I realize that I should have told them, *Don't Touch My Hair*.

Others would say, *Well, why CAN'T I touch your hair?* That question opened my eyes to see what kind of world we live in.

Terreona J.
  Age 11

Moving

It was just a normal day at school when I got the news. The bad news. I was told that I was moving. I was born in North Carolina. That's where I played with friends and cousins playing basketball and doing cheerleading. Life was great. I had a TON of friends but that all came to an end. I was just playing with my friends when my teacher came over and told me that I was moving.

Now don't get me wrong, I was really excited. But I realized that I had to leave everyone. My grandpa got a job here and that's why we moved. Once me and my family got here, we felt like outsiders. We knew no one, and no one knew us. School was the worst. I was the new kid, and I think we all know how that feels. On the first day I made no friends and I was seen as weird but I see why. I started asking kids if killer clown toys were allowed as a joke, but I think they took it literally.

After a while I made a friend. Her name was Jada. We were basically the same person. We started to pretend like we were sisters. We were in the same class the whole school year. I started to feel like I actually belonged. Now I'm going to middle school, and I'm not even nervous. I am so excited to see all of my old friends again.

Tyson A.
Age 11

The Day Covid Happened

The day Covid-19 happened, everybody was at the store and the store ran out of food. The next day I was happy that we got a lot of food. So I was happy because I got to sleep a lot, but I was mad because I couldn't go no where. And I was scared that I was going to get the Covid, and I'm happy now because Covid is almost over.

Tyson A.
Age 11

The Best Dad

My dad is good to me because he buys me stuff I want, and he loves me. And he is a good dad to me. And I think I have the best relationship with him, and we talk every single day. I'm grateful to have a dad like him.

BLACK and PROUD

by Adrian L., Aubrie U., Sevan E., Mianna S., Juliana M.,
Bryson W., Jeffrey A., Joi R., Mikayle H., Saniia F., Sonnie T.,
Terreona J., Gary M., Counselor Erica, and Instructor Devon

I am not perfect, but I will give my very best.
I'm BLACK and I'm PROUD.

They say that there are five steps of grief:
    denial, anger, bargaining, depression, and
    acceptance.
    Well, all of these are me.
    The fact that my ancestors
    been through all of that for hundreds of
    years
    I see a lot of racism go on in the world.

Being Black is hard.
    Being Black comes with a card.
    Some white people treat us like dirt
    over a bag of skittles.
    My life is not finished.

Memories, memories, memories.
    They're the things that define us.
    I should have told them, "Don't Touch My
    Hair."
    That opened my eyes to see
    what kind of world we live in.

Being Black can cause stress, but
  being Black *is* a success.
  I love my good, black hair.
  I love my skin color.

Being Black—is JOY.
  I didn't choose to be Black,
  I just got lucky.
  Never let anyone steal your Black Boy Joy.

I come from a race where
  important people change the world.
  They bring out the best in me.
  My people who are loved.
  My people who are kind.
  My people who are proud.
  My people who blow my mind.

I'll tell you what I am.
  I'm BLACK and I'm PROUD.

Saint Florian Cash Club

———

"To be young, gifted and Black is where it's at!" - Nina Simone

The very first summer I spent working with the Indiana Writers Center, I worked with the SF Cash students as the spoken word intern. I was going into my senior year of college and I was attempting to encourage the students to use their voices and share their light. I remember how we huddled together in classrooms and whispered our poems to each other. They were struggling to express themselves and so was I! So we struggled together and encouraged each other together. That was back in 2015 and that summer was formative for me.

Now in the summer of 2021, things are slightly different. I am getting older and am further removed from pop culture than I'd like to admit. The SF Cash students have patiently explained the proper ways to take a "goofy" selfie and also what certain words mean. I am thankful for their wisdom and insight.

But also, as I have grown in my groundedness and assuredness of who I am, I am seeing those same echoes in the voices of these students. Their vulnerability is unmatched. If they don't understand a writing prompt, they will ask questions of me and of each other. They will press into their insecurities and ask questions of themselves. They are honest and thoughtful, and I can see in them the kind of confidence I did not possess when I was their age.

As we have written together every Monday and Wednesday of this summer, I have been honored to hear stories of their best friends, their fears, their families and their triumphs. So enjoy their words. These brilliant young minds are quite literally our future. They are young (younger than me), Black and proud, and are confident and well-loved enough to know how gifted they are. So drink up their words, maybe learn some new pop culture references and rejoice with me. There is a bright future that is coming. .

Miss Kelsey

Kelsey Johnson
    Instructor

Antonio S.
   Age 14

Insecurities

Since you asked, I'll tell you why I'm insecure. I'm insecure because the way that society is nowadays makes me second guess the way I talk, act, dress etc... For example, back in 2018 I never wore name brand clothes, and very expensive shoes, and had piercings, and never worried about what brand my shoes and clothes were.

Nowadays, all of those things matter to me, and now it's, *Antonio had a glow up*. Now that I worry so strongly about the things that I mentioned, it makes me want to try harder and harder to constantly look better than I did yesterday. And when it feels like I don't, THE INSECURITIES COME! The insecurities lead to depression. Depression leads to self hatred.

Anyiah L.
   Age 14

Life Doesn't Frighten Me

Dear Life,

I have something to tell you. . .you don't put a single fright in my bones. You pushed me through the Devil's fire, snowstorms, car crashes, heartbreaks, mental breakdowns, denials of my existence in YOU! You put me through so much my whole life. You think you can put me down with all the messed up things you gave me as a "lesson to help me through life." Well you have another thing coming. I'm stronger than you think. I'm smarter and more independent. I'm not a quitter, the weakest link in your book of "Life." I'm not going to live the life you want. I will live the way I want. I WILL BE THE MAIN CHARACTER IN YOUR BOOK. I will change the way you work for myself and I will make it through.

I'm young, smart, strong and understanding. I don't have much time to live. I never know when I will die, soon? Never be the straight page with the sharpest edges like the Obsidian knife anymore. Let me live the way I want so I can be happy till the last day I smile, laugh, dance, say I love you to the most dear, to eat my food while not sharing one piece with anybody. So you can hit me with everything from soft blows to much harder blows. I will take them like the champion I am. So back off. Don't test me because life doesn't frighten me.

Anyiah L.
    Age 14

Who Am I?

What do I sound like?
    What do I look like?
    What curious person should know.

A voice like a honey-covered silver flower that permeates through the piercing ice on Pluto. Like a placid, relaxing melody that sways in the atmosphere where only the very special ones can hear. I'm as loud as a lioness that demands to have ner voice be heard far and wide. Underwater or on land, it doesn't matter where, but you will hear. I can be as quiet as an undoubtedly venomous snake that is waiting to pounce on anyone who crosses them. My eyes are like an explorer that's exploring the winter mountains that are blooming with the most beautiful, rare flowers in a meadow full of joy and happiness. My lips are full and round.

Corey G.
  Age 15

Cellular Manipulation

Cellular Manipulation: What I believe to be the best superpower in existence. If you can manipulate cells, then you can manipulate anything since everything has cells/cellular structure. It only works if you know the cells within what you want to control. It comes with a "cell scanner" in your eyes that allows you to scan objects, living and nonliving, in order to get their cellular structure. It also comes with night vision and thermal. The only drawback is that you have to be within a 5 mile radius, look at the object for 3 seconds, and the bigger the object, the more focus required.

Corey G.
  Age 15

Grown Man

When I speak I sound like a croaking frog. Whenever I look at myself in a mirror, which is rare, I notice a Basketball. Bighead. That's it. The only thing about me I don't like is that I'm clumsy and I trip on my own feet more than I should. I have my mom's long eyelashes, my dad's skinny figure and giraffe neck. My younger sister and I both like to laugh at people getting hurt. My oldest sister and I both have a loud laugh, and all my sisters enjoy talking about people. When I'm on the phone with my Grandma Marion, she says that I sound like a grown man. My favorite outfit is an all black shirt with a small Nike symbol in the top left corner, black shorts with white dots that look like paint drops, black and white Kyrie 6's, and my REACTION Kenneth Cole watch I got for my birthday. When I wear that outfit I feel like I'm getting ready to play basketball for 4 hours. When playing basketball I feel sort of creative. I try to make different mixes with moves and shots.

Edosa E.
  Age 14

Good Friends

I met my friend Andru at the YMCA. I was 13 and he was 14. He was in the 8th grade and I was in 5th or 6th grade. We asked each other what's our favorite color, favorite shoes, favorite game, favorite ice cream. His favorite color was black. His favorite shoes was Jordan's. His favorite game was Fortnite. His favorite ice cream was chocolate. My favorite color was green. My favorite shoes were black white Nike's. My favorite game was Fortnite too. My favorite ice cream was strawberry. I think the high school that he is going to is Warren Central High School. I'm going to the same high school that he is going to. I think it's good that me and Andru are going to the same high school because we haven't talked to each other in like a year.

Ja'Len K.
  Age 15

Target Practice

Being Black in America is like having a target symbol painted on my face. I got to constantly look over my shoulder because I know a Karen is holding hate in her heart that is as big as a boulder. Cops ready to empty the clip because they can.

How to get away with murder? Just become a cop. How do they do a home invasion and end with a murder, or a simple traffic stop and end up killing someone and still have their job as a cop?

Ja'Len K.
　　Age 15

Favorite Pair of Shoes

No AJ1 bred, sorry 4s in Columbia blue,
　　But black/cement 3s are the goat Jordan
　　shoe,
　　We probably won't wear them for the fear of
　　creasing or trying to sell "Near DS,"
　　Even though production of them has
　　stopped on the dime,
　　Our love for them is everlasting and will
　　stand the test of time.

Jayden W.
　　Age 14

My Best Friend

My best friend and I met in the 5th grade. His name is Chris. We
have a lot in common. We're both funny, we're both talkative, we
both love playing games, we both like the same rapper artist, etc. We
are still friends and we still go to the same school.

I am in the 9th grade now. I went over to his house to play on his
PS4. Chris is light skinned. He has short hair. He used to have a box
haircut like me, but his mom made him cut it off. He is short and
has a good style for clothes. He has a twin. Only Chris has dimples,
and his twin doesn't. You can tell Chris and his twin apart. His
twin's name is Zion.

We are still best friends and we call each other from time to time.
We started becoming friends on the 3rd or 4th day of 5th grade. He
was cool and had nice taste in clothes. His friends from last year got
the same class as him and on the 3rd or 4th day the class had to do

group work. We were in the same group and we started talking, and a couple days later we were talking a lot and making jokes.

Both of our parents are friends, so we always go to each other's houses. When we go to each other's house we always spend the night. We would usually sleep over each other's house on weekends but, we can't sleep over as much anymore because he moved houses. He moved but he still lives here.

Kaleb K.
   Age 15

Black Joy

Joy: A feeling of great pleasure and happiness.

Joy is expressed through different people through different ways. Some people describe joy as pain, relief, closure... but I was born with this special joy. Joy only understood by me and my people. Black Joy.

Yes, this particular joy was not only named after my skin color, but also my character, culture, and the strong passion and love for my complexion. The sweet smell of grilled hamburgers and brats with a side of macaroni and green beans at the family bbq, or the strong support from my peers screaming my life matters.

Watching the Black Lives Matter protests on my iPhone gave me the motivation and the knowledge that my people are strong. Black Joy doesn't only involve physical pleasure, it is also mental pleasure. The self encouragement I give myself before I walk through the door of life. Or the constant, *I Love YOU, I LOVE YOU,* ramming in my brain while I carry myself, how I want, when I want. I love that I can be who I want and be hated by others in public but also loved by others who share this BLACK JOY in private. The sense of freedom, knowing I can breathe my OWN air. Knowing I can walk wherever

I want and be whoever I want. People try to interfere with my Black Joy, try to sabotage and bring me down, but my BLACK JOY is way too strong and powerful to be tampered with.

My BLACK JOY is hunted unfortunately. It is slowly escaping and finding its way into others that weren't born with it. Being forced through a barrier that isn't meant to be broken. It's converging with a culture, STOLEN, from us. Everything that defines my Black Joy is being broken down, demolished, but I am fighting, WE are fighting to regain our black joy to its full potential. It may not happen today, tomorrow, a year, or while I'm on this earth, but I believe that it will happen.

Kaleb K.
　　Age 15

The Man in the Mirror

What do I sound like? Honestly, I don't know. I'm still listening, curiously waiting for an answer. What do I look like? I mean I know what my physical appearance is. I'm a African American, 5'7, black hair, dark brown eyed male.

But what do I look like? I have no clue. I'm still searching.. Every morning I look in the mirror, waiting to find a reflection but there is no one to be found. I wish I could give you an answer, but I can't give that to you right now. I'm just as curious as you are. Everyone always tells me I look like this or I look like that, but I won't really know what I look like until I discover it for myself. Sometimes I wish I could view myself in a 3rd person perspective to see how I act. To see how I go about my day. I want to see what other people see, but life wasn't made for that so.. I have to do it the hard way. I am trying everything I can to search for this reflection. I surround myself around new people that I usually wouldn't hang around. Or I try new things that I would never dream about doing in my life-time. I leave my home seeking for things that I could do that will help me build this image in my head of who I *really* am. I look at this process as a broken mirror. I find pieces and pieces of this mirror to put together, waiting on the final results. This glass is shattered into 1,000 pieces, and I've only found 1 piece, maybe 2. The good news is I have a lifetime ahead of me to construct this broken glass.

Makail M.
Age 14

The List

I have many pet peeves. There are things like people walking too slow or people driving slow even though I can't drive yet. Other things include talking too much, asking dumb questions, not cleaning up after yourself, not listening, talking during a movie, sagged pants, slow reading, quiet talking, and more. But the thing that bothers me the most is when people smack their food or gum.

I don't know why it bothers me so much, but the noise of it gets me so annoyed. It doesn't bother anyone else in my family, so they do it all the time without hesitation. Even when I tell them to stop they continue doing it anyway. I don't understand how they can handle the noise of loud sounds coming from their mouth. Every single time they eat I have to wear headphones so that I won't have to listen to the noise. I always wonder if I'm the only one bothered by it, but I wish that it would just stop.

Makail M.
Age 14

Self-Love

I LOVE MY LAUGH. . . But when I laugh it sounds like *AHT AHT AHT*. . .especially when I laugh loudly. People say that my voice sounds very business-like and proper. And honestly I don't like my voice. The way it sounds bothers me a lot, all the time knowing there isn't anything that I can do about it.

The way my cry sounds is dead silent, like the noise of being alone in the dark.

My looks....I love the way I look, though there's some things I hate. For example my nose is too big. I hate my smile, and my teeth, and the acne all over my body. I love the way my lips are full like a stomach and the way my eyes look in the sun. They become brighter like honey. I love how my eyebrows are not too thick and not too thin. I love my curly hair as it helps the way I look and completes the circle of my head. I think that everything about me is put together because of course this is who I am.....

That's me, is what I say in the mirror looking at myself....*This is who I am.*

I've been told that my eyes have a lot of depth and soul like the ceiling or having the deepest thoughts. And I agree when I look at my eyes in the mirror it makes me feel calm, like the feel of an empty beach. And the freckles on my face are hardly noticed but they finish me. I love everything about me inside and out from the biggest feature to the things not visible.

Michael D.
    Age 15

Things I Love

Love movies
    Love horror thing
    Love my family
    Love my friends
    Love to imagine things
    Love to pretend

Love going out of town
Love superheroes
Love my parents

Michael D.
    Age 15

Grateful

Being with my family
    That I am here
    That I made friends
    That's it's a new day
    That God woke me

I am happy it's a new day
    I am happy that God woke me up today

Counselor Niki

Fear. What Are You Afraid Of?

People.

People scare me. Not all people. People I know are fine, but it's the people that I don't know that get me. Those people make me hella anxious. I hate going to events where there are a ton of people I don't know. But more so when I'm by myself and have to go.

If I have someone with me then I'm usually okay.

I literally asked my best friend to go with me to two different graduation open houses because I didn't want to go by myself. She didn't know either of the people, but she knew it messed with my anxiety to be by myself so she was down to go with me. In another situation I was going to a friend's house for Thanksgiving. Why I agreed to go initially, I don't know but I had been trying to slowly push myself out of my comfort zone, so I resisted the urge to back out.

On my way to her house I was trying to mentally prepare myself for being uncomfortable. I brought my fidget spinner with me to help calm/distract myself. I thought that I was going to be good...I was not. As soon as I pulled up in the driveway I started to have a panic attack. I was hyperventilating and eventually started crying. I could not calm myself. Then I got mad at myself because I knew my friend and a few other people there so I don't know why I was freaking out. Thankfully I knew the 5,4,3,2,1 grounding technique. ID 5 things you can see, 4 things you can feel, 3 things you can hear, 2 things you can smell and 1 thing you can taste. Eventually after doing that I was able to calm down and go inside.

Once inside I was a little uncomfortable at the beginning, but I got through it and had a really good time. That's how a lot of situations can be for me. But it's getting up the courage and fighting my want to flee that prevents me from getting to the fun sometimes. If you have anxious friends then help them through that. You may see our fears or things that trigger us as irrational. Sometimes we feel the exact same way. We don't WANT to have panic attacks. It's not like we walk around trying to freak out, but sometimes that just happens. Remind them that they're okay or mention the 5,4,3,2,1 grounding technique. Sometimes though the best thing you can do though is to just be there. Just know that we don't do any of that on purpose, and I sometimes get embarrassed. So making a big deal out of it may not help the person in that situation. We just need someone we trust to listen.

Counselor Niki

Ebony & Ivory

Ebony and Ivory are so different

One walks through life stress-free

Not in the sense that they don't have problems but in the sense that they can go about their day without worrying about how people view them.

Ebony doesn't have that luxury. Ebony walks through life with a whole nother type of stress. Everytime they walk into a different space they have to worry about if they are giving off the right vibe.

Ivory and it's meaning is a little bit ironic. When I think of Ivory I think of elephants and their tusks and how they're hunted for their tusks. When in reality it's Ebony that's hunted. They're the ones who have to watch their back and always be on guard like the elephant roaming the desert. Only their desert is a concrete desert.

A concrete desert by definition is known as harshly competitive, unwelcoming or a dangerous place. Which is how Ebony can feel on a daily basis. Unwelcomed each time they walk into a new space. Harshly competitive in the workplace because of the fact that they hold Ebony back from the jump without truly knowing them. A dangerous place because the blue face warriors never seem to really give them a chance. They see Ebony and get geared up for war.

"We learn to live, when we learn to give each other what we need to survive." We need each other to survive. Working together will solve so many issues but people have got to be open and willing. Open like a book, ready to read it and learn about each other. Instead we fight like younger siblings fighting over the remote or the last bag of chips. Like yin and yang...two complementary forces that make up all aspects of life. Yin is the darkness and yang is the light. When not on the same page as one increases, the other decreases. But when in harmony, they work with each other. Without each other they cannot survive. They need each other. Just like Ebony and Ivory need each other. Once they realize that the world will be a much better place.

"Ebony, Ivory, living in perfect harmony"

Preslie-Jai A.
　Age 14

I LOVE ME!

Since you asked, I'll tell you why I'm going crazy inside. I'M GROWING UP TOO FAST. I feel like I was just in 6th grade. Look at me going into high school. 5'0" like an ant compared to an elephant. I know I'm going to have friends, but what if they ditch me? Leave me stranded in a cold, cold world?

Or what if high school breaks me down piece by piece? I've prepared myself from previous people that went through the same stuff as me, but I feel like I have to experience it on my own.

Don't mess with upperclassmen.
　Don't hang around people who do drugs and
　drink.
　Don't turn into a teen mom.

It's a lot to take in. Don't get me started on these middle school boys that you think that you will be together forever. They don't know what they want. One day you guys are in a relationship, the next broken up. Now I know why my mom never wanted me to date at a young age. A boy will flirt with you and want nothing to do with you the next day. I will never understand. I think I wanna stay single forever. Like my gosh. I'm always going to be me though, never going to change up for anyone nor myself. I love me.

Preslie-Jai A.
  Age 14

That One Time

One day on summer vacation with my family we went to ATL because my dad's side of the family lives there. I was younger, maybe 11 or 10. I had this cute shirt on with my back out and some shorts. I was outside playing with some friends and a homeless lady came from out the woods. Keep in mind we are over my aunt's house and there is a trail right next to her house.

So the homeless lady comes with her 2 kids dressed in old raggedy clothes. She comes and asks me where my mom is. She looked at me face-to-face with a black eye and her hair all over the place like she just got beat up. She grabs my arm real tight and tells me, *Come on!*

In my head I'm thinking she's going to kidnap me. But I thought she was going to hurt me so I do what she says. She walks me up to the door. She asked my mom, *Why is she wearing that? Is she a hoe?* While I cry my mom takes me away from her and walks to the car to get a diaper for my brother. Eventually my aunt comes outside and sprays her with a hose.

Later on I went inside my aunt's house and never went back outside by myself again. The homeless lady went back into the woods with her 2 kids while I played Go Fish. I proceeded to tell my mom and dad what happened. The little girls I was playing with left me alone. And my mom didn't hear me cry.

An Anthem for LIFE!

Antonio, Anyiah, Corey, Edosa, Ja'Len, Jayden, Kaleb, Miss Kelsey, Makail, Michael, Counselor Niki and Preslie-Jai

Life doesn't frighten me, nothing at all
    You can chop me by my roots but I will not
    fall

I stand tall and look in the mirror

Being Black in America is like having
    A target symbol painted on my face

I look at all the things that make up who I am

I count them one by one

My family and friends
    Football and swimming
    Amusement parks and fireworks
    My favorite pair of shoes (which are Nike's
    because I like them a lot)

That's me, is what I say in the mirror looking at myself. . .*This is who I am*

But I wonder

Who am I really?
    Do I have what it takes?
    To be bold and be brave
    And to state my case?

What is a superhero?

Someone who saves the world?
Someone who saves themselves?
Someone who's a role model for little boys
and girls?

Who could it be?
    Could it be me?

The world is a big, scary place
    And I am just me
    Life can be tough
    And I am just me

But maybe
    Just maybe
    I can be bold
    And I know I can grow
    And reach my goals

So

I chase my fears away by not thinking about it
    I tell myself,
    We need each other to survive
    I thrive on the drive and the push to keep
    going
    And my joy grows
    My self-love is growing

Because one day
    I wanna tell my grandkids,
    *Your grandparents survived. I learned not to take
    life for granted.*

And

I am happy it's a new day

That's right

Dear Life, I have something to tell you. . .you don't put a single fright in my bones. . .

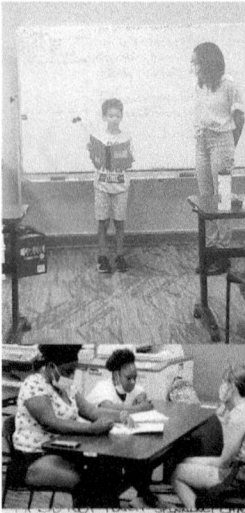

Westminster Neighborhood Services
Youth Services Summer Program

"Come celebrate with me that everyday something has tried to kill me and has failed." - Lucille Clifton

How do you dive into teaching again after being absent from the classroom for over a year due to a pandemic? Will your voice be shaky when you first speak? Will the trusty, old engagement techniques work like they did before? Have you gotten more removed from pop culture? Will you miss more references as your students throw out new vocabulary across the aisle of the tiny classroom?

How do you dive into being a student again? An active learner and participant in the classroom dynamic and collaborative flow? How do you sit at a desk again? Raise your hand and wait patiently? Grip the pencil in your fingers? Press the dark lead against the faint blue lines? Is there fear? Excitement? Anticipation? Boredom?

I can answer all these questions with a simple yes. Yes to all of this. All of this will most likely happen and more questions and doubts will arise. And as we, the interns and instructors from the Indiana Writers Center, walked into Westminster on the first day of our summer session, I knew we would be facing a mountain of some sort. The students were walking in with so much. They are young and deeply entrenched in technology (they know more about TikTok than I could possibly fathom). They have watched with their own eyes as this country reckons with race, class, healthcare and more. There has been so much death over the past year. I was nervous. Would they want to talk, to share? Would they be willing to be vulnerable?

I had been in their shoes before, in this classroom before. Last year they were not necessarily so willing. Last year we pushed and they pushed back. But this year, they opened. And with the opening up of their minds, their imaginations and their hearts, there has come so much magnificent writing.

Every Monday and Wednesday we gathered together and they shared something with us--stories, laughs. We were grateful. From tales woven about pet lizards and their favorite rappers, to the time they had their first heartbreak, to the people they love and dearly miss, these Westminster students were vulnerable with us. Being vulnerable at any age is not an easy feat, but these young writers have given us their trust and we do not take it lightly. We've played games and learned new slang. We've eaten snacks and made some memories.

I am filled with gratitude to know that in between their busy Westminster summer schedules of reading programs, field trips, gardening and more, they spent a little time with us, telling their stories. You'll find their words in these pages and I encourage you to soak them up. They are imbued with joy, astute observations and a whole lotta truth.

Celebrate their vulnerability with me. Celebrate their triumphs and their passions. When these children speak, they make waves and when they decide to act, the ground will shake. I've seen that much and I am so proud.

Miss Kelsey

Kelsey Johnson,
  Instructor

Amiyah W.
    Age 10

Zion, the Twerk-A-Nator

Something that made me laugh was when we were at Westminster playing tag in the dark when Zion got on the bookshelf and started twerking. And it was a 2000/10, and I was laughing so hard that I fell over and I was rolling over.

Amiyah W.
    Age 10

The Day I Broke Someone's Heart!

One day at my old school, in the middle of recess, my ex came over to me and asked me to get back together. But I rejected him and when my boyfriend heard him he ran over to me and hit my ex.

Amiyah W.
    Age 10

New Friends

One day it was my first day at my new school and when I was in the hallway walking to my 3rd grade class I saw my new teacher. When I walked in she welcomed me with a warm hug. She is so nice. I love seeing her at the end of the day. :)

The second day I met my best friend Samya. She saw me and I was all alone at lunch and she walked over to me and started to talk to me and we became friends that day. A few weeks later we were now best friends. We have been best friends for a year.

A'ron D.
    Age 12

How I First Met My Dog

One day my mama call me and my sister and my mama told me to get the food. Me and my sister came and my mama came in the house and open her coat and it was a pitbull with green eyes! And my mama gave it to my sister and my dog peed on her and me. And my sister was happy and my mom name him Melo and I love playing outside with him. We do not take him for walk because we got a backyard.

A'ron D.
    Age 12

Someone I Miss

I miss my mama because she take care of me and she keep a roof over my head. She the best mom ever. She buy me everything. So when I go home she still at work and when she off work we go out to eat and I love her so much. I care for her.

Braylon W.
    Age 13

My Dog

We were in love with dogs because my uncle had a bunch of them. Then the dog we called brown dog had a litter and we got to choose one and we named it Edna the pitbull and it was a female. We took care of it until it was 2 because we weren't around and dogs need a lot of attention. So we gave her to another family with a lot of kids so they could get the attention she deserves. Also my sister cried all the way home. I felt bad but I knew that it was good for her. She was wild and she loved my mom.

Braylon W.
   Age 13

Someone I Miss

My grandpa was a hard working man and always worked on his lawn and I helped him when I was younger. While he mowed the lawn I picked up the sticks. I loved my grandpa. I used to be around him a lot when I was a baby and a bit older but then we stopped going there after a while. Then we continued to going there when I was about 11 and 12 but then he died because of lung problems since he only had ½ of his lungs. When he died I felt numb.

Cayden C.
   Age 13

My Day

wake up
   take a shower
   clean self
   put on clothes
   get on phone
   play my game – 2k
   eat
   lay down
   watch youtube – mr. beast
   and then go to sleep.

Cayden C.
   Age 13

Peeves

A list of things I can't stand is when my brother gets in trouble and I get blamed for him. I would try my best to be good but still get in trouble. Something else I can't stand is when I go home then my dog just start begging me to walk him when I just got there 3 minutes ago. Something else that irritates me is when the Internet goes off and I'm bored. Life is better with Wifi.

Counselor Christina

Losing A Friend

I really miss my best friend, [ ]. They were and still is my best friend of about five years. They are tall, curly haired, and a bit rowdy. We hang out all the time here at Westminster, where we met. At first I didn't really like or care for them since I thought they were mean and rude. *Well,* I mean they can be mean and rude but never in a serious manner. I think I met them in the fall back when I started fifth grade. They are about a year older than me but the two of us were in the same grade. Eventually over time I started to get closer with them and became friends. We laughed and joked with each other. They would tell me stories about school or what happened in their life. I would listen and chime in from time to time. It was fun and nice. This was and still is the longest friendship I ever had with someone.

That's why I never expected to not see them for so long. It's been about three years since I last said goodbye to them. It was the summer before sophomore year. We had worked together side by side here at Westminster. It was the last day so Westminster had a full day of celebration going on. We said goodbye with a promise of working together next summer. But that didn't happen, and with no way to contact them I had essentially lost any and all connection to them. I remember crying myself to sleep because the pain of losing someone that close to me was too much to keep in. I used to hope that one day they would come back and at least say hello, maybe even exchange numbers to reconnect. But I've sort of given up on the notion, not in a *I don't think I'll ever see them again.* More as in *if I ever do see them again, I'll make sure to never let them go again.* I have a way of seeing people I haven't seen in years even if they don't remember me.

So I'm cautiously hopeful that I'll just see them while out shopping or doing something mundane. And if I don't I'll just remember all the good times we had together.

Colby H.
   Age 13

My Day

The day I changed about the things I do everyday that are like spending less time on video games during the day, and watching TV more. But me as a person I can do way more than those things but it's so much to say, for me it's like I wanna do more stuff. Before those things I start my day by brushing my teeth, then, fix me some breakfast with just some cereal, next I watch TV for 3 hours long or for 4 or 5 hours, it depends on what I'm feeling in the mood for. Finally I go on my computer and watch Youtube for almost the rest of the day and then I stream on Twitch for the night then it's back to the start.

Colby H.
   Age 13

The Story of How Me And My Best Friend CJ Met (Year 2018)

It all began with me just playing the Xbox watching Youtube. And then all of a sudden my friend Taeshawn invited me to a party and turns out there was another person in there which was my friend CJ. It all began when Taeshawn was bullying him and I just couldn't let that happen so I told CJ to add me and talk to me and ever since that moment he was like a older brother to me because he helped me see to not take life for granted and helped me to fix friendships. So yea, I love my friend.

Corbin L.

Age 8

My Pet Peeves

When I ride a wet roller coaster and my
shoes and socks get wet.
Someone getting bullied.
And when I play Fortnite I get spamed.
When I play Mortal Kombat with my sister's
boyfriend and he wins.
When my mom gets in a car traffic and I'm
in it.
When my sister hits me then I tell my mom
and she said she didn't do it.
When I get on a wet roller coaster and it
doesn't get me that wet.

Corbin L.

Age 8

My Best Friend is Malik

We have been best friends for a few weeks. We met at camp.
When we met I came up to him and we started talking about what
we were going to do that day at camp. Then we started becoming
friends. Lunch came and we played together. We like to play stuff
we just make up, like stuff we like to talk about. He talks to me
about his mom and how she's getting a degree and a big new house.
We want his mom and my mom to get each other's numbers so we
can go over to each other's houses. He's funny, nice, caring, and
helpful. He helps me with things sometimes. One time he helped me
read a book during reading time. I'd like to go to Skyzone, swim-
ming, and Zip City and play with Nerf guns with him. I'm happy to
be best friends with him.

Cristina B.
Age 12

My Lizard

A story that happened to my lizard, Seattle, was like a year ago. My lizard had torn up his blanket, so he wasn't used to not being covered while he sleeps. He decides to bury himself under his log for comfort. He kept moving around the log while I was asleep and I guess it fell on his tail and it hurt too much for him to move so he slept like that. Once it was morning, it was his shower day because he gets weekly baths. I try to pick him up, not knowing it's pulling his tail. He flares up at me, and I get scared because he's not the type of lizard to get mad. I found out what was wrong and his tail like bent. Over the past 2 weeks we treated it and was told by vets his tail is going to eventually fall off. It did. After this happened, my mom called him stumpy :)

The End.

Cristina B.
Age 12

My Day

I wake up. I brush my teeth. I play with my lizard. Sometimes I call my lizard Washington because his name is Seattle, so it goes together. If I was in school I would go to school. People might notice that I don't talk to people because I only talk to my lizard. I like staying at home a lot.

I have realized that I'm an introvert. I don't like to talk to many people. I have a social battery and I'm nonchalant. So if I get tired of you, you will know, and if I feel a certain way about someone. I also watch shows that are 1 season and like 8-10 episodes because I have zero patience.

Daja R.

Age 12

Best Day Ever

Since you asked, I'll tell you why I was happy today. I went to the creek. The water was super strong that it even pushed me back but I did get back. Then we rolled all the way down the hill and the hill was steep. After we went to the park there was a big slide and when we came back they had ham sandwiches but I couldn't eat it so I had extra grapes and pretzels. Then I did gardening and had a scavenger hunt. That is why I'm happy about the best day ever.

Daja R.

Age 12

Things I'm Scared Of

1. Snakes
2. Spiders
3. Breaking bones
4. People following me
5. Driving

But the scariest thing of all is my mom. I hate upsetting her because she does a lot for me and my brother, and if you went to my house you'll see, it's toy city. And if you stacked all the toys up it would be almost as big as a Christmas tree! I hate when I upset my mom like when I lost my computer that I needed to bring to school and if I did not find it, it would cost $800! I found it and everything was fine. But this is why I hate upsetting my mom.

Elyjah L.
Age 12

Things I Love

A list of people and things I love:

- My Dad
- My game, Fortnite
- My cat, Max
- Pizza
- Cheddar Cheez-Its
- Rap music
- Playing games

My dad is nice. He is a preacher at Patoka Church. We go out to eat and we go to church. He makes me laugh all the time by making funny faces. He bought me a Fortnite gift card which I loved.

Elyjah L.
Age 12

Since You Asked

Since you asked, I'll tell you why I'm happy. I'm happy because I'm at Westminster camp. We go swimming, go to the park to play basketball, get on the swings. I enjoy going to the Splash Pad and hiking the most. We always play tag. My friends are Cayden, Prince, Braylon, and Amiyah. We always have fun together at Westminster.

Gabrielle T.
Age 8

Girls Are Strong

One day I started at my new school, Our Lady of Lords. I was sitting in math class and Gabe, he said something about our gender. I kind of heard him say *Girls are useless*. When I heard that, I got up from my desk and yelled at him in his face and asked him *What did you say?* My friends Coco and Ireland helped me calm down and they tried to cheer me up. They helped me but I was still crying and screaming at Gabe. Then Gabe was called out of the room for 5 minutes by our principal, Mr. K. When he left the room, I calmed down.

Gabrielle T.
Age 8

Family YouTube

Me and my mom are planning to make a
    Youtube channel.
    On first Day my mom
    On second Day me
    On the third Day little Brother
    On fourth Day my Dad
    My mom will be cook Filipino food.
    I am going to be playing Roblox.
    I don't know what my brother and dad are
    going to do.

Hayven B.
Age 14

Me

i take naps twice a day. for no reason really.
i just get really tired.
i eat everyday. i'm pretty sure I'm supposed
to though.
i don't eat much.
i'm near-sighted.
pencil sharpeners are loud.
i'm bored.
i watch youtube all the time.
i write my 'a's weird.
i can't spell very good. i'm not good at
grammar either.
i wanna take a nap.
i also wanna go home.
whoever's reading this. *How's life?*
hope it doesn't suck.
i like to play games.
like minecraft and cs:go and osu! and
overwatch n' stuff.
it's hard to play some games cuz my laptop
is slow.
people
i don't like them that much
some people are loud & annoying
some people underestimate how much
i don't care
but that's not the topic
my brother is 6'10
i'm a compulsive liar
i've probably told quite a few lies today
i told somebody i'm bad at mobile games

i'm not.
i told someone i liked their hair
i didn't.
i told someone i was bad at math
i'm not.
dang i lie a lot. x
my sister told me
nothing
i have no idea why i wrote that
why do i keep skipping lines
how has it not been 15 minutes yet
i don't like barbecue chips
i'm black and i wear black all the time
i don't know why i wrote that either
i think the teachers read these when
we're done.
if that's the case ignore the compulsive liar
thing and don't judge me.
i'll kick you through the paper
i need to charge my phone
but i'm socially awkward

Hayven B.
Age 14

Things I Fear

I'm supposed to write about fears and I don't want to. Colby has a Junji Ito shirt that's cool.

Anyways, idk what I'm scared of. Just normal things like being judged or killed or shunned.

How long do I hafta write for? :(

More things I fear

- Bring judged.
- Death.
- Pain.
- People that unironically wear red Among Us and think it's funny.
- People who like Twizzlers.
- People who eat without their mouth closed.
- I'll probably be scared of my high school teachers.
- Boring books.

I'm just naming things that I don't like at this point. New list.

- People with bass in their car.
- People/office workers that wear dresses.
- People with long fingernails.

That's just a lie. I'm just gonna name random things.

- Reading.
- Minecraft.
- Some Roblox games.
- Cabinets.
- Spelling.
- My grandma's flip phone.
- Resident Evil games.
- I like animals.
- Reptiles :D.
- Writing.
- Strings that come out of my clothes.
- Bad tasting water.
- America.
- Obama cared.
- Humans.
- Explaining myself.

Lemme list a few categories that list just went by.

Things I...

- don't like.
- think are fun.
- like.
- despise.
- am okay with.
- think are old.
- get bored of quickly.
- and some more.

It's not in an order, but it's all there.

Lamonte C.
    Age 14

ANNOY

When people be disrespectful to me I feel sad or not like myself. One time I was at home and I had my cousins over and they annoyed me, disrespected me. When I told them to clean like it was clean when they got there, they messed up the downstairs. And I said, *Clean it up before I get in trouble* and *I have to take y'all punishment from my mom.*

Lamonte C.
    Age 14

Play All Day

When I was 12 or 11 when I was in the house I was watchin' TV. I was watchin' TMNT (Teenage Mutant Ninja Turtles). I was on the couch watchin' it and I was eating, taking naps and playing with my Legos for about 30 min. Then I went outside and play with my friends, then 15 min later we went into my friend's house and we play and talk. Then after 30 min later I went to ride my bike in the

2nd neighborhood for the first time. I like riding my bike in the 2nd neighborhood because it is bigger.

Malia C.
    Age 11

Pressure

When I stump my toe, I apply pressure to it.
When I say I apply pressure, I mean, I step
on my toe with all my body weight.
I do this because, it helps it feel less,
hurtful. I check to see if it's bruised by after,
I apply pressure. My mom always tells me I
shouldn't do it.
How I got the idea of Applying pressure?
I got the Idea from the TV shows on Netflix.
It all started when I found out about *Grey's
Anatomy.* When you bleed out, you apply
pressure to fix the bleeding. I also got
the Idea from *Vampire Diaries*. They
stopped the bleeding with a cloth,
so I use my foot.

Malia C.
    Age 11

My Laugh

Here's my big laugh.

It was July of 2020, my friend Cayden, recommended a show called *Vampire Diaries*. She said, *The characters are very funny and cute.*

If I was to watch it, W*ill you leave me alone?* I asked.

It was horrible. There's this character Damon who had great humor. He would say things that were dark and funny. I was in the living room. The lights were dim. I was on my gray couch with my pillows and my cat. I was watching season 6 episode 18, Damon and Alaric were looking for the invisible house. Damon turned and saw Jeremy, Elena, the main character's, brother. He had a crossbow.

Damon then says, *C'mon Jeremy.. put the crossbow down, Pochahontas.* I laughed so hard, It made my stomach hurt. It may not seem eye-watering, stomach-hurting, but when you're alone at 1 am, everything's funny.

Malik R.
   Age 13

My Best Friend Corbin

The good days I've had with my best camp friend Corbin are when we hang out and help each other. We like to talk about stuff like action and adventure movies, games, and life. We are always defending each other and playing together. Our favorite thing to do is laugh about what comes first. We vote on the same things when choices are given. An activity that we do is Basketball where I can shoot the ball with one hand perfectly.

Malik R.
   Age 13

Things I Can't Stand

1. Talking bad about me.
2. People not taking situations seriously.
3. Spamming in Roblox, Mortal Kombat, Street Fighter.
4. When I can't help others.
5. When things are left in pockets for laundry.

When I was young, 2 people had got mad and started fighting me. They were twins and they had took something I wanted. I took it back and that turned into a fight. They hurt me but I got back up, and from that day on I learned to slow things down and how to fight.

Malik R.
  Age 13

The Future

Since you asked, I'll tell you why I'm excited. My mom is working on her nursing degree and is passing all her tests. She will get her degree in September or October. When (*not if*) she gets her degree, she will buy a big house with a pool and go-karts. I'm debating on if I should get a dog, cat, or parakeet. Each will have a name to describe them: Sausage, Tuna, and Mr. Chicken. I will teach the parakeet to fly in my sister's room and say, *What's up kid?*

Nevaeh L.
  Age 9

Things I Love

 1. Mommy
 2. Daddy
 3. Attention
 4. Running outside
 5. Saying, *What in the world?!* and *What in tarnation?!*
 6. My Little Pony toy called Applejack
 7. Pepperoni and cheese pizza
 8. My Little Pony YouTube videos
 9. Christmas… I like presents
10. Pink!

I love My Little Pony. It is my most favorite show ever. It makes me laugh. I like when the ponies go on adventures. My dad bought my Applejack Little Pony for me. It was a surprise! I play pretend with Applejack. It is my favorite pony. Well, I have another: Rainbow Dash. Rainbow Dash is a pegasus with blue fur and a rainbow mane. Applejack is orange with yellow hair. I wish that I could be a pony!

Nevaeh P.
    Age 12

Me and Sky

One day me and my sister was at my grandma's house and we was about to leave and my sister looks down and finds a turtle.. So we told our grandma and grandpa and they said we can keep it. So what we did was we took it in the house and put it in a bowl of water and took it to the pet shop. When we got to the pet shop we got the things for it and took it to my house to set it up. We get to my house and we decide to put it in my room because I had more space than my sister. So we started to set it up and put water and rocks and filters and etc. So now I have a cute turtle named Sky.

Nevaeh P.
    Age 12

My Favorite Rapper

One day I needed some new music in 2019. I looked on my trending page and Pop Smoke's song "Flexin'" came up. I listened to it and I immediately went to Youtube and played all of his recent music. By the end, I was in love with him! But on February 19, 2020, Pop Smoke was shot and died. When he died I was really devastated, but tried my hardest not to show it.

Prince C.

Age 8

Cartoon Cat and Mr. Dot Team

Two years ago I got my cats, Cartoon Cat and Mr. Dot. We got them from my therapist's friend. The friend's cat had kittens, which is how we got Cartoon Cat and Mr. Dot. They were very tiny but they're big now. Mr. Dot has white and black dots. Cartoon Cat has mittens on her. They're silly and hyper and kinda lazy. One time, I gave them catnip, but they got a little bit too crazy.

Cartoon Cat and Mr. Dot always fight because they're brother and sister. When they fight, they make weird noises like a cow. After they fight, they fall asleep in the cat house that we built for them.

They have toys, like this big giant thing they can chew on and eat. We play together too. I get the stick with feathers on it and they follow me when I walk. They don't bite or scratch much, but if they do, it doesn't hurt. One time I tripped over them and I SCREAMED bloody murder and they did, too. I love my cats, they're very good.

Prince C.

Age 8

Best Day

I went to the water park I got a bite But then
    I went on the swing
    After I went home I was mad But my nana
    and papa
    Calmed me down we was Home I rushed
    inside
    Then I put on my pajamas on then I played
    on

My laptop finally I fell asleep
Next day I woke up
Then I Brushed my teeth
After I ate a pancake
Then I went to daycare

RJ G.
Age 13

Skate Fun

This past Sunday my mom dropped me and my sister off at WOW's
(Wheels of Wonder) to go skating. When we was there I got a
Mountain Dew Icee and ate pizza. Skating is easy because I go
almost every Sunday. I go faster than my sister because I rollerblade
and I like to rollerblade. Sometimes I stay 3:00 to 9:00 pm. I like to
dance in the middle. I can also jump, spin, go backwards, and
crouch.

RJ G.
Age 13

My Favorite Places and Things to Do

My favorite tv show is "Young Sheldon". It's funny, smart, and it's
about a kid named Sheldon who is a germaphobe. He is short and
nice. He lives in Texas. He had two friends. You need to watch it
because it's good and a lifetime story.

My favorite movie is *Twilight*. My favorite character is Edward. He is
protective over Bella and is smart. He is a good friend and he is nice.
Bella and Edward are high schoolers. It's about the girl and the
vampire (Edward) getting married but the vampire tries not to bite
the girl.

My favorite place is the mall. My favorite store is Finish Line. My favorite shoe is the Black and Red Jordans. I go to the arcade. I play the racing and claw machine for tickets. I like going to the food court and getting a Chick-Fil-A sandwich. I got a double chicken sandwich, fries, and a coke. It is the downtown mall. I also like to go to the Eagle Hideout (Eagle's Nest). The top spins around and it's a restaurant. I got salad, chicken, bacon, and cheeseburgers, fries and a coke.

Samya R.
Age 10

Broken Heart Candy

So I'm going to tell you when my sister broke my heart. She had some candy so my sister gave my mom some candy and I said, *Can I get some?* And she was like, *wait until we get home* so we drove 30 minutes home. And we got out the car and came up the 8 stairs to get to the house and we came upstairs to my room. My sister went in her room. So then I knocked on her door and she opened the door and I saw the candy on her bed. So I said *Can I get some?* And she said, *get what?* and I said— candy— and she said, *I don't got none.*

So I went back in my room and I took a nap then I woke up about to get my fan and she came out her room eating the candy I wanted so I was like *Can I get some now?* And she said sorry that was my last one I was like .... Dang. *Can you guess what candy was it?*

Samya R.
Age 10

I Am Going To Tell You Both

So I am going to tell you a story of someone I miss. So I had this best friend and her name was Breair. And her mom had some stuff going on in Indianapolis, she had broken her neck and other stuff and so they moved to Atlanta. And me and my sister got their phone number off of TikTok messages so now we can call them. But the fun part is that they are coming back in December for Christmas and if we are not out of town we can go and see them! When we was on the phone we were shy but we had really missed each other. I am going to tell you about when I met my best friend. She was a new kid at Westminster and she didn't have no one to play with so we came downstairs and we played with her. But at first my sister didn't like her but then she got used to her and that's how I met my best friend Breair.

Saniy R.
   Age 11

Travelin' Places

Something good that happened during the Covid year? Was that me, my sister, brother, and mom were traveling during the summer. The places we went were Kentucky, Wisconsin, Illinois. It was really fun to spend time somewhere else and with family. In Kentucky we went to my cousin's grandma's house to celebrate his birthday. In Wisconsin we were at a hotel and a pool, and an amusement park. In Illinois we went to go visit family, we were watching TV and talking about old times. I felt good.

Saniy R.
   Age 11

The List of Saniy

- Family
- Cheese pizza
- TV
- TikTok
- Nice shoes
- Myself

- Swimming
- Red
- Purse
- Honesty
- Jayda
- Amya
- Tomariana
- Purple Doritos

When I get in the pool I like it and know to swim very good. That's why I love swimming. I taught myself how to swim.

Counselor Shaay

Sirrrr!

Something good that had happened COVID year is me getting my Shih Tzu puppy named Sir. I bought him from the craziest place but I wanted to risk it. It was a website called Craigslist. I got him in September first and beforehand I was annoying my friends, counting down them days to get him because he was too small. Eventually I got him when he was 5 weeks old. He was so small, he was able to fit in my crocs and had a lot of space to move. He was so small for his little legs that he used to hop everywhere. I miss him that small but now he's about to be 10 months and he's still small.

Counselor Shaay

Missing Houston

Something I miss is Houston, Texas.

Why am I back from Houston you may ask?Because life and I mean adulting life was kicking… I mean punching me in the face. It's hard being a full time student and then working to pay bills and survive. I'll be back soon. What I miss is:

The heat

The constant sun glaring in my face making my skin look immaculate.

The palm trees blowing in the fresh breeze here and there.

The beautiful melanated people to easily meet and network with.

The different foods/restaurants from different ethnic groups to try.

Always having something to do when I'm bored.

Having a strong sense of comfort and feeling welcomed everywhere I go.

Having the ability to visit different parts of Houston and feeling like you're in a whole new city.

Being able to break out of my shell and try new things.

Not having to worry about seeing people I know because Houston is so big.

Seeing the beautiful sky towers at night

3 more semesters left until I'm officially reunited with Houston for good.

"BE SOMEONE"

Sheila G.

Age 14

My Day

Hi, I'm Sheila and I'm going to tell you about how my day goes, really. I'll sleep till afternoon or middle of the day then I wake up, check my phone, then I go back to sleep. Clearly you can tell my sleeping is way off but it's my Life. And when I get up, I check my Snapchat or Insta and that is kind my whole day, so yeah.

Zion K.

Age 9

The Best Barbecue

One really good thing that happened last year was that my cousin came over for a barbecue. My cousin is a couple years older than me. We brought the barbecue to the pool. We played hide-and-seek because we didn't know how to swim. I always win. We ate regular hot dogs, beef hot dogs, hamburgers, sausages, and brats. There were barbecue chips, plain, Lay's sour cream and onion. I didn't know how to swim but I stayed in the parts of the pool I could stand in.

Zion K.

Age 9

Quarterback and Point Guard

Since you asked, I'll tell you why I love football. I love catching the ball and running really fast to get a touchdown on the other team. Every time I get a touchdown I do my touchdown dance, "The Right Foot Creep." I play the quarterback position.

Since you asked, I'll also tell you why I love basketball. I am an all-star! I am a point guard on offense and I block on defense. When I play basketball I always dunk on people. It is easy for me to dunk and hang on the rim and break people's ankles.

Zyllah L.
  Age 10

TikTokers vs. YouTubers

Since you asked, I will tell you why I'm angry. I'm mad because I didn't get to see the Tiktoker vs. Youtuber fight. I wanted the Tiktoker to win But I knew Austin McBroom was going to beat Bryce Hall. Bryce Hall was talking all that stuff but got beat up in the boxing ring. I couldn't watch the livestream BECAUSE YOU HAD TO PAY. 😑 Bruh

Zyllah L.
  Age 10

What Scares Me

Getting yelled at
  Sharks in the water
  My Grandpapa's house at night
  Ghosts
  Tsunamis
  Haunted house
  Kidnapped
  I'm scared my Grandpapa's house because
  all the lights be off at night .
  I'm scared ghosts because why not?

A Year with Westminster, A Summer of Writing

by A'ron D., Amiyah W., Braylon W., Cayden C., Colby H., Corbin L., Christina V., Shaay M., Cristina B., Daja R., Elyjah L., Gabrielle T., Hayven B., Lamonte C., Malia C., Malik R., Nevaeh P., Nevaeh L., Prince C., RJ G., Samya R., Saniy R., Sheila G., Zion K., Zyllah L. and Intern Jess

Well, we haven't done anything explicitly to celebrate our accomplishments for the past year, but we have done some things.
We talked about...
Lego Ninjago
SPICY RAMEN (noodle) SQUAD
Edna the Pitbull
Nana's pet Hunter
Pop Smoke
Cartoon Cat and Mr. Dot
Young Sheldon
We celebrated our friends and family...
I love melanated people.
I stay until the streetlights come on with my
friends.
My best friend is CJ.
My best friend is Malik.
My best friend is Corbin.
My best friend is Breair.
I was at my best friend's house, and we
decided to do a slip and slide in the kitchen.
I was so excited!
We struggled (just a little!)
:/ Bruh
But it's my life sOo...
duh duh duhhh!!!
I miss my mama because she take care of me.
I'm not afraid of horror movies.
Life is better with Wi-Fi.
I wish I could watch people write.

I am going to be playing Roblox.
How long do I hafta' write for?
But overall...
Something good happened during the Covid
year,
Something amaaaaaaaaaaaazing!

Appendices

Writing Prompts

———

Below find the writing prompts for each of the three sites we served this summer. We share these prompts with you in the hopes that you will join our community of writers and write your own stories. Remember, your story matters!

Horizons Program at Saint Richard's Episcopal School: Writing Prompts

Playlist of my Life:

- A song that reminds you of your family
- A song that reminds you of your friends
- A song that makes you think of summer break
- A song that makes you think of the holidays
- A happy song
- A sad song

Now choose ONE song from your list:

- Does a song transport you to a memory of a specific person, place, or event?
- What did things look like, sound like, feel like, smell like, sound like?
- Who was there? What did you do? What emotions did you feel?

Who is the trickster in your life? What are some of the things they do that make you laugh? What are some of the funny stories they have told you or that you remember about them? If there is not a trickster in your life, what is the funniest story you have ever been told? How hard were you laughing and do you still laugh today when you think of it? What is the best joke you have ever heard?

Tell the story about what happened when you were mean to someone or someone was mean to you.

Describe the most colorful place you've ever been. Tell the story of something that happened there.

Describe your favorite pair of shoes and tell the story of something that happened while wearing them.

Read aloud the poem "Where I Come From" by George Ella Lyon. Now tell the story about where you come from OR write a poem modeled after Lyon's poem.

Tell the story about what happened when you had to do the hardest thing you ever did.

Read aloud the poem "Honey, I Love" by Eloise Greenfield. Make a list of things and people you love. Write a poem how you came to love one of those things or people.

Tell the story about what happened when a day went differently than you expected it to go.

Read aloud the poem "Life Doesn't Frighten Me" by Maya Angelou. What scares you? What doesn't scare you? Make a list of the things that scare you. Write a poem/rap about what scares you OR write a poem/rap about how you chase away your fears.

Tell the story about what happened when a new person came into your life.

Tell the story about what happened when you were the new kid in a place where everybody else knew each other.

Write a letter to your future self. Do you have any regrets to apologize for? What are the dreams and goals that you're most excited about? What advice do you have for yourself?

Saint Florian Center Youth Leadership and Development Center Summer Camp: Writing Prompts

Saint Florian JC (Littles) and Core (Middles)

Tell a story about a time when you celebrated your Black girl or Black boy joy.

Write a letter to someone not born yet about COVID-19 and tell them what you learned, what it was like, and what should be remembered.

Read aloud "Things I Always Do" a poem by Mason Smith, age 14 from *The Best Teen Writing of 2016*. Begin by writing: 'Sometimes we can learn the most about one another from the average everyday things we do...' Tell a about the everyday things *you* always do. What can others learn about you from the things you always do? Tell me the story of a time when you noticed something new about yourself because of the things you always do.

Tell a story about a time when someone told or made you feel like your black life did matter.

In the middle grade book *One Crazy Summer* by Rita Williams-Garcia, three young black girls in Oakland watch their mother get arrested. In the aftermath, a friend and neighbor, Mrs. Woods, comes over to help the girls, saying, "We know the same things. We have to stick together," (178). Tell a story about a time when a family member, friend, or neighbor took care of you during a difficult time. What did they do for you? How did it feel?

Tell the story about what happened when you lost something (or someone) important to you.

Tell a story of what happened when a new person came into your life.

Tell a story about what happened when you had to do the hardest thing you ever had to do in your whole life.

Describe a place you love and tell a story of something that happened there.

Tell a story about what happened when someone did something to surprise you.

Tell a story about what happened when something or someone really scared you.

Describe a person you love and tell a story of something that happened when you were together.

Saint Florian Cash Club (Bigs)

Start your spoken word poem with the line, "Since you asked, I'll tell you why I'm _____ (angry, worried, scared, in love, sad, hopeless, fearful, etc.)" Use the prompt to give us your best rant.

Write a poem about your Black joy. What does Black joy feel like to you? If it was a color, what would it be? If it was a place, where would you go? What does it sound like? What does it taste like? How does it feel to you?

Read aloud "Life Doesn't Frighten Me" by Maya Angelou. Write a poem/rap about what scares you OR write a poem/rap about how you chase away your fears.

What do you look (or sound) like? What do you like about the way that you look? What do you not like about the way that you look? Why? Write a poem using as many metaphors/similes as you can. Use adjectives, hyperbole and personification too!

Make a list of things you can't stand or things that are your biggest pet peeves. Write a poem about one of those pet peeves.

Think about your best friend and how you met them. Write a poem about/for your best friend. What do you want to tell them? How do you want to encourage them and celebrate them?

Imagine what the world will be like when the pandemic is over. Free-write a letter (in the form of a spoken word poem) to someone not born yet--a cousin, a brother, sister, your own future child, a firefighter, a health care worker, essential care worker--anyone, really.

Tell them what this time was like, what you learned and what you think should be remembered. Share your hope for what the world will be like when (sooner or later) the crisis is over. Be as specific as you can be.

Westminster Neighborhood Services Youth Services Summer Program:
Writing Prompts

Great go-to's for when you are "stuck" or "don't know what to write about".

- Since you asked, I'll tell you why I'm_____ (angry, worried, scared, in love, sad, hopeless, fearful, etc. . .)
- Tell the story about what happened the first time you. . . (whatever).
- Describe nothing. If nothing was a color, what would it look like? If nothing was a sound, what would it sound like? Taste like? Feel like? What sort of candy would nothing be? Keep asking questions in that vein to help them stretch their minds.

Read Aloud "Things I Always Do" a poem by Mason Smith, age 14 from *The Best Teen Writing of 2016*. Sometimes we can learn the most about one another from the average everyday things we do. Tell me about the everyday things *you* always do. What can others learn about you from the things you always do? Tell me a story of a time when you noticed something new about yourself because of the things you always do.

Tell a story about something—an event, a friendship, a family--good that happened this past year (during COVID).

Tell a story about what happened when something made you laugh so hard your stomach hurt--or worse!

Make a list of things you can't stand or things that are your biggest pet peeves. Tell a story about how one of those became your pet peeve.

Tell a story about something no one knows about you.

Tell a story about how you, your family, or your community gathered, celebrated, mourned, and/or recognized accomplishments in different ways this past year (during COVID).

Since you asked, I'll tell you why I'm _____(angry, worried, scared, in love, sad, hopeless, fearful, etc.)

Draw a map of your neighborhood. Put an "X" where something happened that you will always remember. Write the story of what it was.

Tell the story about a favorite memory with your favorite pet.

Make a list of things and people you love. Tell a story about how you came to love one of those things or people.

Tell the story about what happened when you broke someone's heart OR when someone broke yours.

Read aloud the poem "Life Doesn't Frighten Me" by Maya Angelou. What scares you? What doesn't scare you? Make a list of the things that scare you. Write a poem/rap about what scares you OR write a poem/rap about how you chase away your fears.

Tell a story about a time when you felt tough and brave.

Is there someone you miss or lost? Tell a story about that person.

Tell the story about how you met your best friend.

Editor, Designer, and Instructor Biographies

Editor, Dr. Darolyn "Lyn" Jones — Dr. Darolyn "Lyn" Jones serves as the Education Outreach Director for the Indiana Writers overseeing the Building a Youth Public Memoir Program. Lyn is also an assistant teaching professor in the Department of English at Ball State University. Lyn is passionate about literacy, story, and social and educational justice and has committed her thirty-one years of professional life to those topics. She is the educational author of a top selling series book titled, *Painless Reading Comprehension*, co-author of *Memory Workshop* with Barbara Shoup, the editor for a digital literary magazine, *Rethinking Children's & YA Lit: Read for Change*, an editor for the children's book series, *The Neon Tiki Tribe*, an editor with the Indie 409 Press at Ball State University, and one of the editors of this Indie Press, INwords Publications. Lyn has edited, authored, and published multiple creative narrative nonfiction essays, memoir anthology collections, and scholarly articles surrounding race, community engagement, and disability including *Monday Coffee and Other Stories of Mothering Children with Special Needs*, Where *Mercy and Truth Meet: Homeless Women of Wheeler Speak*, *Keep Muncie... Wierd and Whimsical*, "Sitting at the Feet of my Flanner House Elders: A Lesson After Dying," "In Indy, #BLACKYOUTHMATTER," "Unschooling Teaching Practices and Community Literacy," "Mother-Teacher-Scholar-Advocates: Narrating Work-Life on the Professorial Plateau'," and this, the 10th volume of *I Remember: Indianapolis Youth Write about Their Lives.*

Andrea Boucher is the book designer for Indiana Writers Center and design editor for Booth, the literary journal published by the Butler University MFA program. With over twenty years of professional experience in the publishing field, she's done it all: author management, copy editing and proofreading, book design and layout, project management, and print/publication consultation. In addition to her design work, she also teaches at Butler University and is a writer with multiple publications.

Sarah Seyfried is a writer and editor. She recently graduated from the IU School of Liberal Arts at IUPUI where she earned a BA in English. As a student, she acted as Vice President and Managing Editor for *genesis: Literature and Art Magazine.* She has also interned with *Indianapolis Monthly* and worked with IUPUI as a web writer and editor. Her published work includes "Mannered Rejection," which received an ICPA award in the "Best Formal Poetry" category. This is her first year with the Indiana Writers Center.

Danilo Almeida is a current double major in biology and creative writing at IUPUI who is also pre-dental. Danilo is originally from São Paulo, Brazil, and moved to the United States at an early age. In addition to his majors, Danilo is also involved at IUPUI as the president of the performing arts club, a resident assistant, an editor for genesis (IUPUI's student literary magazine), and a researcher at IU's School of Dentistry. He hopes in the future to become a dentist but still be involved in the writing field by writing children's novels and assisting with teaching young kids English.

Kelsey Johnson is an actor, writer and educator. She received her BFA in Acting from Ball State University, graduating cum laude. After graduating she continued her education as an acting apprentice in the 2016-2017 Professional Training Company at Actors Theatre of Louisville. She is currently based in Indianapolis where she balances her time as a teacher, professional actor and the occasional spoken word poet. She has been working with the Indiana Writers Center since 2015, but she has also worked for the Indianapolis Shakespeare Company, Conner Prairie, Indy Reads bookstore (through their AmeriCorps program) and as a classroom theatre teacher.

Nykasia Williams is a rising senior at Ball State University studying Psychology and African American Studies. After graduating, Nykasia plans to attend Graduate school to earn her Masters in Youth and Family Counseling, with hopes to one day open her own Mental Health Rehabilitation Center. She passionately advocates for marginalized voices through research and public memoir projects. This is her third year as an intern for the Indiana Writers Center and continuously looks forward to sharing the stories of our youth.

Emily Mack (lead instructor at Horizon's) is a graduate of Ball State University, where she studied English Education and Creative Writing and tutored at the Ball State Writing Center. Her writing has appeared in *Turnpike Magazine* and *Knots Undergraduate Journal of Disability Studies.* This is her sixth summer with Building a Rainbow. Emily now teaches middle school literature in Greenwood, Indiana.

Devon Lejman is an advocate for the power of storytelling in classrooms, in workshops, and in her own life. In 2020, she graduated from Ball State University Magna Cum Laude with a BA in English Education. Devon is thrilled to be in her third year with the Indiana Writer's Center's Building a Rainbow program and co-instructing alongside her former professor, Dr. Lyn Jones. Along with teaching young writers, Devon writes personally and professionally as a way of making sense of her world. She teaches high school English in Anderson, Indiana.

Acknowledgements

———

The Indiana Writers Center's Building a Rainbow Youth Public Memoir Program gratefully acknowledges the support of these organizations and individuals for their contributions and time.

Executive Director
Rachel Sahaidachny

Writer in Residence
Barbara Shoup

Education Outreach Director
Dr. Darolyn "Lyn" Jones

Program Director
Sarah Ginter

Site Instructors

Kelsey Johnson, Dr. Darolyn "Lyn" Jones, Devon Lejman, and Emily Mack

University Student Interns

Danilo "Danny" Almeida, Hailey Beaty, Emily Badger, Kat Doan, Carlin James, Sarah Seyfried, Jessica Walls, Mikayla Vaughn, and Nykasia Williams

Volunteers

Mary Redman and Celeste Williams

Organizations

Allen Whitehill Clowes Charitable Foundation
Suzanne Plesha & Ball State University Immersive Learning Office
Goose the Market Owner Mollie Eley and Staff
Horizons Program at Saint Richard's Episcopal School (HRES)
Lilly Endowment, Inc.
Saint Florian Center Youth Leadership and Development Center
Summer Camp
Teachers' Treasures
Westminster Neighborhood Services Youth Services Summer
Program

Individuals

Lauren Brown and Michael Brown
Angela Jackson-Brown and Robert Brown
Ariana A. Cagle
Penny S. Craig
Kaitlyn Daily
Justin Hauter
Jim Jones
Renee and Jim Jones
Cassidy Langston
Devon Lejman
Betsy Lewis
Mark Liley
Tracy Mishkin
Elaine Orr
Mary Redman
Kathy Thomas
Sondra Ward
Celeste Williams
Sharon Williams

www.ingramcontent.com/pod-product-compliance
Lightning Source LLC
LaVergne TN
LVHW051403080426
835508LV00022B/2948